Reading Difficulties and Dyslexia

Reading Difficulties and Dyslexia

An Interpretation for Teachers

J.P. DAS

$\circledS$SAGE Los Angeles • London • New Delhi • Singapore • Washington DC
www.sagepublications.com

First published in 2009 by

SAGE Publications India Pvt Ltd
B 1/I-1 Mohan Cooperative Industrial Area
Mathura Road, New Delhi 110 044, India
www.sagepub.in

SAGE Publications Inc
2455 Teller Road
Thousand Oaks, California 91320, USA

SAGE Publications Ltd
1 Oliver's Yard, 55 City Road
London EC1Y 1SP, United Kingdom

SAGE Publications Asia-Pacific Pte Ltd
33 Pekin Street
#02-01 Far East Square
Singapore 048763

Published by Vivek Mehra for SAGE Publications India Pvt Ltd, typeset in 10/13pt AGaramond by Star Compugraphics Private Limited, Delhi and printed at Chaman Enterprises, New Delhi.

Third Printing 2010

Library of Congress Cataloging-in-Publication Data
Das, J.P. (Jagannath Prasad)
    Reading difficulties and dyslexia: an interpretation for teachers / J.P. Das.
        p. cm.
    Includes bibliographical references.
    1. Reading—Remedial teaching. 2. Dyslexia. I. Title.

LB1050.5.D355   371.91'44—dc22   2009   2008048186

ISBN: 978-81-7829-895-5 (PB)

The SAGE Team: Rekha Natarajan, Prashant Gupta, Anju Saxena and
                        Trinankur Banerjee

For Gita
my counsellor, companion, wife

Contents

III. The Next Steps

List of Tables

List of Figures

Epilogue

Notes

List of Abbreviations

ADD	Attention Deficit Disorder
ADHD	Attention Deficit Hyperactivity Disorder
ARD	Average IQ Reading-Disabled
CA	Chronological Age
CAC	Chronological Age Controls
CAS	Cognitive Assessment System
COGENT	Cognitive Enhancement Training
CTOPP	Comprehensive Test of Phonological Processing
FAS	Fetal Alcohol Syndrome
fMRI	functional Magnetic Resonance Imaging
FN	First Nations
MA	Mental Age
PASS	Planning-Attention-Simultaneous-Successive
PET	Positron Emission Tomography
PREP	PASS Reading Enhancement Program
RAC	Reading Age Controls
RAN	Rapid Automatic Naming
SACC	Student Activity Completion Checklist
STM	Short-Term Memory
WIAT	Wechsler Individual Achievement Test
WISC	Wechsler Intelligence Scale for Children
WRMT-R	Woodcock Reading Mastery Tests-Revised
ZPD	Zone of Proximal Development

Preface

Dyslexia and "poor reading" can be distinguished by assuming that dyslexia is a specific reading difficulty whereas poor reading is a general one. However, the distinction is not always strictly maintained in this book. Both terms essentially refer to reading difficulties. "Reading Difficulties" is used as a general term to identify children and adults who struggle to read and comprehend what they are reading. However, some of them may not have any difficulty in listening comprehension. Their difficulty may be specifically related to reading, which is converting written words to speech. Decoding letters to their corresponding sounds, and learning how to pronounce different parts of the word, especially unfamiliar words, are extensions of the same problem experienced by dyslexics. The teacher can test how well or poorly a child with dyslexia can read, but the reading test would not tell her/him if there is an underlying deficit in "phonological" processing, which involves converting a written word to its components of sound. This is explained in the first few chapters of the book.

Beyond phonology (converting written words to speech), there may be broader cognitive deficits. For example, difficulty in sequencing, what comes after what—when asked to spell "push", the dyslexic child cannot tell if the word begins with "b", or if the letter "u" must precede "sh". This is the usual difficulty in successive processing. Do these children have low intelligence, and therefore cannot read? The answer certainly is "no". Dyslexics and children with reading difficulties, who cannot decode words, are found at all levels of intelligence, ranging from low to high. Comprehension, on the other hand, may be partly associated with low levels of intelligence, but not in all cases. This is further explained in the chapter on comprehension.

This book is an interpretation of dyslexia and reading difficulties in terms of the underlying processes. It gives the reader a condensed source of current knowledge. So far as theory is concerned, the book interprets the topic in terms of PASS (Planning-Attention-Simultaneous-Successive) processes, that is, the four major processes of knowing and thinking that replace traditional views of IQ and redefine intelligence. These ideas are elaborated in special chapters in the book.

Reviewing the contents of the book, basic questions, such as what is dyslexia and how do reading difficulties develop, are answered in Part I of this book. How do I deal with dyslexia? Is there a valid remedial procedure that I can use? These questions are central to Part II. Part III briefly looks at ongoing concerns regarding reading difficulties that have not been covered in detail elsewhere in the book. Finally, the Epilogue presents a brief review of new developments in research on dyslexia and reading difficulties. The Notes elaborate the ideas in a chapter, and for some chapters make the contents come alive with practical examples. For some other chapters, they offer clarification of issues that were too complex to deal with in this brief survey.

The book is not an exhaustive scholarly discourse on dyslexia and reading difficulties. It is intended to be like a sampler menu offered in a gourmet restaurant: You can view the full menu but only have time to dip into a few select dishes.

For the school psychologist, this book is an interpretation that gives preeminence to the PASS theory of cognitive processes and their assessment. Specifically, it uses PASS theory to explain "unexplained reading disability", that is, reading problems that are not explained by a traditional IQ test. Typically, when a teacher refers a reading-disabled child to a psychologist for assessment, the results may do nothing more than confirm what the teacher knew all along—that the child has normal or better than normal nonverbal ability, but significant weakness in verbal ability. The teacher puts the report aside with a sigh, and continues as best he or she can to teach the child to read. The book goes a step further by offering remediation programs, which are derived from the theoretical framework of PASS.

PASS theory has gained popularity and now its battery of assessments, the Das-Naglieri Cognitive Assessment System (CAS), is being used with confidence in several countries for general assessment as well as for assessment of special children. In English or in translation (Spanish, Italian, Chinese, Japanese and Korean, as of this year), CAS is used for diagnosis of the underlying cognitive deficits of dyslexics and poor readers. This book demonstrates how the PASS theory and assessment can answer the question: What do I do following the cognitive assessment of children with reading difficulties? The answer is important not only for guiding remediation, but also for understanding the nature of the specific reading problem known as dyslexia.

The book provides a brief but authentic discourse on topics that are vital to understanding the continuing enigma of dyslexia. What is phonological awareness and how can it be placed within the context of cognitive processes? Is dyslexia due to a block, an embolism as it were, in the course of the natural flow of reading progression from symbolic to orthographic stages of reading? Can neuropsychology expand our understanding not only of reading but also of spelling and writing? And finally, is there a rational basis for remediation that is supported by both cognitive psychology and neuropsychology?

Neuropsychology takes the school psychologist back to the structure and functions of the brain that are constantly evolving as a result of the experiences of the individual in school as well as through experiential learning. The book will be perceived by school psychologists as having a theoretical bias, but this should not interfere with existing knowledge; rather, it ventures into the frontier regions of the field, searching for explanations and solutions in the broad beam of a theory's flashlight.

Before completing the preface to the book, I want to discuss two major problems that challenge the teachers and school psychologists and are a cause of frustration for the parents. The first problem is the child's reluctance to write. The second is related to understanding or comprehension—how can we help children to improve comprehension.

Writing

Writing has become a problem with many children, including schoolchildren in India. Teachers complain about it because some children refuse to write. If even in examinations they are turning in a blank answer sheet, should the teachers fail the student and deny promotion to the next class?

There are two important phases of writing, early childhood and a later phase after age 10. What could be the major questions, in both phases and specific to each phase?

The mechanical part in writing includes simple skills such as holding the pencil or the pen, proper formation of letters, and leaving space between words. These are the basic skills in handwriting. Many children hate to write because they are generally clumsy. They may not have a good control over their fine movements and coordination of hand, fingers, and the eyes. Usually many of these children have no neurological or physical reason for their clumsi-ness. They were forced to write when they were not mature enough, at ages three and four. They pick up bad habits of writing because they cannot cope with the fine motor skills that handwriting requires. If left alone, and if they are not taught handwriting until they are above five years of age, many of them will find it easier to write, and even take pride when they have learnt the skills for handwriting.

By the age of 10, schoolchildren have mastered the skills of writing and the simple rules of punctuation and grammar. Also, with the possibility of typing on a computer, the mechanical part in writing will not pose a problem. In fact, most children who hate writing will benefit if computers are allowed in the classrooms and examination halls. More information on writing is given in the chapter on spelling and writing as well as in the notes on that chapter.

We read to know. We write to express. This is a simple fact, but teachers and parents may not remember this. The second phase of writing is all about expressing thoughts and feelings, intentions and emotions. Even as an adult, it is difficult to express one's thoughts accurately in writing. There is a gap between the intention or desire to communicate something and subsequently putting it down on paper. Emotions and feelings are not always adequately represented in writing. We cannot express in writing everything that we perceive, and we certainly cannot express adequately what we feel. Help children to improve their writing by asking them to imagine as if they are talking to another person who cannot see them, who cannot hear their tone, or see their face and gestures. Then, continue to write.

Learning to read and write in two or three languages even before children are six has become a major difficulty for children in some countries. The problem is so serious, that it is a hindrance in making children literate. This is especially so in Indian schools, which begin to instruct in English at preschool.

Teaching for Comprehension

A serious consequence of forcing children to read and write in two or three languages, before they have reasonably mastered their mother tongue, is poor comprehension of what they read. Current newspapers in India have pointed out over and over again that schools in primary grades emphasize rote learning at the expense of comprehension. This is all the more harmful when using a second language (English) as the medium of instruction in the schools. Teachers and parents may not realize the big difference between reading English and reading any of the other languages, such as the Sanskrit-based ones (Hindi, Oriya, etc.), German and Greek—children make more mistakes in English reading because the letters do not always correspond to sounds (for example, the letter "a" is pronounced differently in "apple" and "ace"). If you read inaccurately, you cannot understand well.

But there is hope for enhancing comprehension. We have encouraging results of using PREP, the remediation program (see PREP chapters in the book); we show how comprehension deficiency can be easily corrected in a short period of time by using PREP. Try to use the core elements of PREP in classroom instruction, especially when teaching bilingual children, for whom it seems easier to learn vocabulary by rote than comprehend the foreign language.

The core elements of PREP tasks improve comprehension; some evidence is presented in the chapters on PREP. Comprehension skills increase in children through *abstraction, perception of inter-relationship among the obtained information, strategic thinking and the ability to focus on relevant information to the exclusion of the irrelevant ones.* The children are also encouraged to become *aware of their use of strategies through talking to themselves* while solving a problem. This is specially helpful for those who are weak in planning strategies.

I can only hope that many teachers and school psychologists will find the book's contents useful. They will also appreciate the value of research and its application in teaching reading. A long line of my former students have contributed to the ideas and studies in this book and continue to enrich my knowledge in reading. Notable among them are Professors John Kirby, Rauno Parrila, Timothy Papadopoulos, and George Georgiou, the youngest one in this group—a long line indeed, for George was not even born when John completed his PhD with me.

J.P. Das

I

Understanding Reading Difficulties

1

Good and Poor Readers

Dyslexia is a word that is often used for poor reading ability. The word has its origins in Latin and Greek: "dys", as in dysfunction, meaning "difficult", and "lexis" meaning "speech" or "word". Thus, it is a useful word for describing a very specific reading difficulty. Poor reading is too broad and too vague a term and could be reflective of a number of factors including those associated with poor environmental conditions such as malnutrition, disease, widespread illiteracy, or poor schooling and instruction. Dyslexia, on the other hand, is more limited and specific, and can be used to specify a reading disability associated with *an inability to translate written language to speech*. The dyslexic child may not learn to read easily and may not be able to write the words that he/she hears. These difficulties in converting written material to speech and spoken words to writing are the essential characteristics of dyslexia.

As we shall see, in this and other chapters, reading ability develops early, normally during the first or second year of schooling, and it goes through certain well-defined stages. Therefore, dyslexia can be hard to detect before reading instruction begins formally either at school or at home. By the end of the second year in school, it becomes clear if a child is experiencing difficulty in reading and spelling. This may occur even when the child is receiving adequate instruction. Speaking develops naturally for most children, but reading has to be taught. Learning to read, therefore, is the most important task that children face during their first two years of school. With proper instruction most children learn to read easily.

Dyslexics are a Class of Special Children

Special children are those who need special attention in education and healthcare. The special children we find in schools nowadays include all children with special needs, whatever their handicap may be. They may be intellectually impaired or slow in learning. They may have one or another kind of language difficulty, or simply be slow in development. Other children may have sensory impairments, for example, hearing difficulties or visual limitation, or other medical conditions such as epilepsy and brain damage. Very often, teachers are called upon to pay special attention to these children in the classroom. The teachers want to know the medical, physiological or psychological causes that produce sensory and motor defects, language impairment, immaturity, clumsiness, and different levels of intellectual impairment. For many years the so-called medical model was used to treat special children, that is, the child's condition was thought to be similar to a disease which could be cured, preferably by medication. That idea was discarded 30 or so years ago when it was realised that all children need to be educated according to their ability. Some educators still believe, however, that a teacher does not need to know the cause of a child's handicap, that the teacher is there to teach, and his or her best course of action is to determine the entry-level skills of the child and then begin to improve upon those skills. Other teachers maintain that a thorough knowledge of the various barriers to learning that they might encounter in the classroom will expand their expertise and direct them in designing the most appropriate special instruction for these children.

For example, the teacher will want to know if the learning-disabled child lives in a community and family that does not benefit from books, educational media and interactions with literate adults. Other children with a learning disability may have difficulty in intellectual processing or may suffer from a neurological impairment. Thus, it is best to consider all the conditions, medical, physical, psychological, and cultural, in understanding those children in the classroom who need special assistance (see Figure 1.1).

A mother called me about her 4-year-old son. She was worried that he might be dyslexic. He seemed to be very clever, spoke

Figure 1.1   Special Children: Who are They?

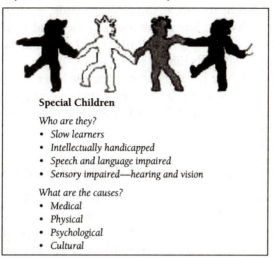

Special Children

Who are they?
- *Slow learners*
- *Intellectually handicapped*
- *Speech and language impaired*
- *Sensory impaired—hearing and vision*

What are the causes?
- *Medical*
- *Physical*
- *Psychological*
- *Cultural*

Source: Author.

and understood as well as other children of his age, but both his father and uncle were diagnosed as dyslexic in primary school. Would he take after them? Were there any early signs that she should be watching for, and how soon could remediation for dyslexia begin?

She was right to be a little concerned. Approximately two-thirds of dyslexic children are boys. Dyslexia does sometimes run in families, potentially increasing the risk of a child developing the condition. What should she look for that might reassure her that her son is not likely to be a poor reader in school? First, she should ask herself the following questions:

- Does he speak in sentences?
- Can he follow a sequence? (She can test this by asking him, for example, to open the cupboard and take out all the old bottles, then to remove all his crayons and papers from the table and put them away, and, finally, to repeat her instructions.)
- Does he find it easy to say words that rhyme? (She can make it a game: "Tell me a word that rhymes with *cat*", or "Which word does not belong to the group: *boy, toy, bun, coy*?")

She can play other word games with him as well. For example, she can ask him to repeat unfamiliar words, such as *Pretoria, Veracruz, Wabamun*. She might also ask the child to keep saying the words *tiger, bus, egg*, in that order and as fast as he can, over and over until she tells him to stop.

She can also help her son to recognize the letters of the alphabet by using plastic magnetic letters on the fridge door. If she still has any worries at the end of the first grade, she should take her son for assessment.

Dyslexia: How to Recognize it? How Common is it?

In this and the following two chapters, the characteristics and diagnosis of dyslexia are discussed in detail. But, how common is dyslexia? The answer to this question varies widely, depending on how we define dyslexia and how we identify it in a child. Estimates of the occurrence of general reading disabilities in elementary school range from 10 percent to 20 percent, but dyslexia as a true defect in the intellectual makeup of the child may be as low as 2 percent. Far more boys are dyslexic, as compared to girls. There are several possible reasons for this:

1. There may be some biological factors that make male children more prone to dyslexia.
2. Girls generally possess superior language skills and these skills develop more quickly than they do in boys. This may compensate for any initial handicap girls might have in learning to read.
3. Boys are often harder to handle in the class than girls, so the teacher is more likely to notice them.
4. Boys tend to be less interested in reading and much more interested in acquiring physical skills, such as cycling or hockey, because culturally, in many communities, reading is an activity for girls.

Reading is a cultural activity and is a good example of cultural learning. In a community with a low literacy rate, there is neither the need nor the opportunity to learn to read. However, lack of schooling is not to be confused with illiteracy. A rural community that does not have a formal education system can nonetheless be highly literate, demonstrating great appreciation for its rich oral traditions such as knowledge of poetry and scriptures. In such a community, the opportunity for acquiring reading and writing can be successfully introduced. Many traditional and rural societies in India or China are able to catch up with reading and writing when formal schooling is introduced through adult-literacy programs. The critical element seems to be a literary environment and facilities that sustain the practising of elements in literacy.

How do Children Learn to Read?

Learning to read is the most important task that children face during the first year of school. Whereas speaking is natural and develops naturally for most children, reading has to be taught. In spite of good instruction, however, many children fail to learn to read by the end of their first year in school. Many reasons are given to explain why they fail. Two commonly held beliefs are (a) a lack of exposure to printed or written material, and limited experience with reading material in their daily environment, and (b) the child has a delay in her/his development or has a specific deficit in intellectual skills which affects the ability to transform spelling to speech. Without this ability to transform the written word, reading is inhibited from being an automatic activity. Such children read laboriously with great effort instead of reading fluently. Typically, reading fluently appears to be second nature at the end of the third year of formal instruction at school.

Learning to read is a process that passes through several well-defined stages. Briefly, children begin by reading short words as though they are pictures. In other words, they are not aware of the relationship between the letters or syllables and their sound. Thus words such as *man*, *cup*, *boy* and *girl* form a whole picture that children read by sight. The word *bus* is visually similar to *bush*, and children at this stage of reading may be unable to distinguish between the two.

As their reading progresses, they encounter unfamiliar words that they cannot read by sight. They break these words down into segments and sound them out (*an-i-mal*). Thus, though they are unaware of how they are reading or what processes they are using, children read familiar words by sight and unfamiliar words by sound (see Chapter 2).

Reading is not simply a matter of identifying words; it also involves comprehension, that is, understanding the words in context. For many years educators did not separate word decoding from comprehension, but treated them as one entity called reading. But it became clear that some schoolchildren can read but have difficulty in understanding and, conversely, others cannot read but have no difficulty in understanding passages that are read to them. (Children with dyslexia fall into the latter category.) As a result, today word identification (decoding) and comprehension are treated as two separate processes.

The dyslexic child's inability to convert spelling to speech can be observed by any teacher. Additionally, deficits may exist in certain intellectual skills, such as the ability to put things in sequence or to follow the sound patterns in a word. In general, these children lack the cognitive processing that is essential for breaking down words into an ordered sequence of sounds. This kind of skill is at the heart of what is called "phonological coding" or "phonological recoding" and is discussed in the next chapter. For the time being, let us accept that there are two main causes believed to be associated with reading difficulties:

1. A specific intellectual or cognitive processing difficulty that is at the root of phonological coding.
2. A failure to learn to read due to a variety of external as well as internal conditions, which may include the child's inability to profit from instruction where the standard of instruction is poor, and the inability to pay attention during instruction.

Garden Variety

It is recognized that there are two types of poor readers—*Garden Variety* and *Dyslexic*. 'Garden-variety' poor readers show intellectual or cognitive processing problems in many areas, and not only in putting things in sequence as already discussed. They may also experience problems in seeing relationships among words, objects or pictures, in sustaining attention, and/or in the ability to organize and plan ahead. In a garden there are all sorts of plants, including weeds, and it is difficult to organize them in any specific order. What grows in the garden might not fit into any particular order or category, and we could say that the reasons for the garden variety of reading difficulties are similarly mixed. Within this group are children who are culturally disadvantaged, that is, books and reading materials are not commonly available in their culture. There are those who lack motivation and role models for good reading; this is the case in communities where most children do not go to school but start working as soon as they can, from the age of seven or eight. Also there are many children with emotional and sensory problems, such as difficulty in hearing or in seeing (hearing impaired or visually limited), who are likely to be poor readers. Thus, we have to revise our set of causes for garden-variety poor reading—not all causes involve intellectual deficiency. Some of the children may be perfectly adequate in terms of their intellectual and cognitive functions but do not have the cultural advantage of urban middle-class children in a "print-enriched community". Within a few months of being exposed to a literate environment, such children overcome their reading difficulty and may begin to learn to read well.

In contrast to the garden variety of poor readers, there are the dyslexic poor readers who show specific deficiencies in only a limited number of intellectual or cognitive processes. The most important deficit, as mentioned before, concerns the ability to sequence, that is, to put sounds and words in order.

Thus there are three kinds of poor readers: (a) those who have some disadvantage due to an external factor, including poor instruction; (b) those who have a general cognitive deficit; and (c) those who have a specific deficit in only a few of their cognitive or intellectual functions.

Good Readers Read by Sight and Sound

Who are the good readers then? Most children, about 85 percent, learn to read with relative ease through proper instruction. The stages of reading, as discussed earlier and further in Chapter 3, begin with children reading short words as though they were pictures, that is, they are not aware of the relationship between the letters or syllables and their sound. A word such as *bath* may be visually similar to the word *bat*. A child who reads the whole word as though it is a picture may not be able to distinguish between them.

After three years of reading instruction, reading becomes an automatic process. Good readers read almost all familiar words by sight, although they are not aware of how they are reading. However, when they are reading fluently, they will sound out unfamiliar words. Research into reading shows that familiar words are read by sight, whereas unfamiliar words are read by sound. So a child may read the words, *man*, *cup*, *boy*, or *girl*, by sight—as a whole picture—while at the same time spelling out new words such as *tied* or *cobbler*. When a child is breaking down a word like *cobbler* into segments he/she follows the sounding of the word, for example, *cobb-ler*. These points will be discussed again in the next chapter.

Word Identification and Comprehension— One or Two Processes

Sometimes we read words in isolation, but mostly we read them in a sentence. Often the sentence is a part of a paragraph which tells a story or discusses an idea or an event. Therefore, although reading a single word is the beginning of all reading, even the child in Grade 1 is given words to read in sentences and gauges their meaning from the context of the sentence. Recognizing a word by itself is important, but understanding the word in its context is more frequently demanded. No wonder reading includes both reading a word in isolation as well as understanding the word in context. However, for many years we did not separate word identification, or word decoding as it is called, from word comprehension. We thought that reading meant just recognizing a word and understanding it within a context. But then it became clear that among schoolchildren, there are some who can read but cannot understand, and then there is an opposite group, those who cannot read but have no difficulty in understanding words or sentences read aloud to them. Facts like these have forced researchers to consider word identification (word decoding) and comprehension as two separate processes. There is no doubt that it is possible to assist the first group to understand by having someone read the word or sentence aloud to them, and teach the second group to read fluently.

Dyslexia is not Word Blindness

Many years ago educators and medical practitioners believed that dyslexia was a case of "word blindness". This was especially evident when such children were asked to track a sequence of written words with their eyes and were often found going back and forth over the same sequence. This was in contrast to children who read normally and who tracked the string of words smoothly. It was assumed by eye doctors who diagnosed the condition that children who were dyslexic had some kind of visual impairment. In recent years, however, this belief has been shown to be unfounded and, as a result, research has turned to a multilayered examination of the processes involved in learning to read.

There is a consensus that although a small number of children with dyslexia may have some sort of visual problem, the vast majority of them have none. For the vast majority, the most important difficulty is in phonological coding, that is, in the conversion of written letters and words to sounds, especially when the words are unknown or are "made-up" words, such as *bom* or *tept*.

Beyond Phonological Coding

In this chapter it is suggested that we should look beyond phonological coding and consider the fundamental cognitive processing that may be of critical importance in acquiring reading skills among beginning readers and especially among the population with dyslexia. We suggest that the process that lies beyond phonological coding is a difficulty in sequencing, in appreciating the succession of letters within a word and of words within a sentence. Therefore, a rational method for helping the child who has dyslexia should begin with facilitating successive or sequential processing. (These are discussed in Part II as an integral part of PREP.)

There are many tasks that might be structured to enhance successive processing. One method consists of exposing the child to tasks where he/she is required to attend to a sequence of shapes (a triangle followed by a circle, then a square, a rectangle, a trapezium, and so on) and to reconstruct the sequence after a short interval.

The same successive processing can be imposed on letters such as *c-o-b-b-l-e-r* that are presented in an irregular array. The child's task is to draw a line connecting these letters forcing him/her to pay attention to their sequence. This is discussed further in Part II along with many other suggestions about tasks to facilitate successive processing.

2

From Nursery Rhymes
to Phonological Coding

Children first learn words by listening to them and only later by reading them. Listening discrimination, that is, accurate discrimination between two similar sounding words is learnt through day-to-day experience. We have observed, for example, that children as young as three who grow up in an English-speaking environment, but in a household where the parents' mother tongue is not English, soon begin to correct their parents' English diction. While children acquire a foreign language very easily, it is not the same with parents, who may be unable to reproduce words exactly as they are spoken by the native speakers of that language.

As listening discrimination is developed through incidental and planned experiences, parents and educators can assist its development in children. One way is through the pairing of words that differ only in one speech sound, for example, *bad–bat*, *tap–tat*. The child is asked to identify the difference in sound. There are other interesting ways of making children pay attention to the difference between closely sounding words. We could put two different dolls in front of the child and say, "This doll says *bad* but this doll says *bat*. Which one says *bad*?" Or, using the same dolls—"This doll *ate* and this doll *eight*. Which doll *ate*?"

An important consideration when addressing difficulties in listening (auditory) discrimination is the elimination of a possible difficulty in speech perception. This is why auditory discrimination tests are useful in detecting whether or not the speaker is engaged in appropriate phonological coding. Phonological coding can also be tested by tasks that test phonological awareness.

Phonological Awareness can Predict Reading Skill

First of all, what does phonological awareness mean? Essentially, it is the ability to translate letters into sounds or phonemes. A phoneme is any of the units of sound that distinguish one word from another, for example, *m* and *c* in *mat* and *cat*. Phonemic awareness includes grapheme–phoneme correspondence, which is the ability to pronounce phonemes that are printed. The following are some of the important ways of estimating a child's phonological awareness:

Identification

Ask the child to tap every time a different phoneme (sound) can be heard or read in a word. Ask the child to tap the number of syllables in the words *put*, *potty*, *nut*, *nutty*, *span*, *separate*, *dance*, and *return*. Similarly, ask the child to say *here* and *hen* and then ask where in the word does the *huh* sound occur. Continue by giving words such as *where*, *free*, *sat*, and *paper*, and ask which one has the sound *er*.

Phoneme manipulation

Ask the child to take away the first sound from the words *phase*, *star*, and *get*. Similarly, ask the child to take away the last sound of the words *water*, *flat*, and *gap*. Then ask the child to take away the middle sounds in words, for example, the *b* sound in *table*, the *n* sound from *window* and the *eh* sound from *bread*.

Sound blending

Provide the sounds that constitute a word and then ask the child to put it together: *a–ni–mal*.

Children's performances in tests of phonemic awareness as well as rhyme detection help predict the level of reading ability. However, what is more important is that in pre-readers, the results predict children's success in reading in later years. Therefore, experienced teachers and educational psychologists who do research in reading emphasize that children should be encouraged to create the sound of the word from its printed form and, conversely, clearly spell out spoken words. The separation of the sounds in a word and the appreciation of the sequence or succession of these sounds is beneficial for teaching how to read.

Children spontaneously generate rhymes, even nonsense rhymes, by the age of two-and-a-half. They just love making songs that have no meaning at all but which bristle with rhymes and alliterations. Rhymes usually refer to words with endings that sound the same, whereas alliterations are words that have similar-sounding beginnings (Peter Piper picked a peck of pickled pepper). We know that rhymes are easier than alliterations for children to detect. Just think of some of the more popular rhymes for children found in the books by Dr Seuss, *They play all day, they fight all night*, or others such as *Mr Brown went to town* and *Jack Sprat could eat no fat*.

Children also notice how hard it is to pronounce groups of words that have both alliteration and rhyme together, as in *She sells sea shells by the seashore*. Considering the same example, children also become aware of phonemes as easily as rhymes and alliterations. We do not have to teach them sound discrimination formally if they are exposed to word games. In fact, much of language is learned through play. Language learning is a serious affair; to paraphrase Jerome Bruner's remark—some things are so important in life that they can only be learned through play.

Let us summarize the main thoughts about phonological awareness or phonological coding (see Figure 2.1):

1. Remember that the terms phonemic awareness, phonological awareness, and phonological coding are sometimes used interchangeably. All of them refer to the ability to translate letters and patterns of letters into phonological forms. This ability includes what is called the grapheme–phoneme correspondence, that is, the ability to pronounce phonemes that are written down.

2. Not only are single letters pronounced, but also groups of graphemes and groups of phonemes have correspondence. For example, b-e-a-d is *bead*, but b-r-e-a-d is pronounced differently. Hence, it is not always easy to pronounce whole

Figure 2.1   Tasks for Assessing Phonological Awareness

Phonological awareness, or phonological coding, can be measured in several ways. In tests of phonological coding we include items from each of the six types of task listed.

Tasks usually used:

- Rhyme production or nursery rhyme tasks
- Oddity tasks
- Blending tasks
- Syllable splitting tasks
- Phoneme manipulation tasks
- Phonemic segmentation tasks

Source: Author.

words in a foreign language although we can certainly pronounce each letter. A name like *Krywanuik* certainly involves the translation of groups of graphemes into groups of phonemes, but if you do not know the language such correspondence is never accurate. Try explaining to a person, who does not know English, how to say *minute* in *wait a minute* and *minute details*.

3. The ability to translate letters or patterns to sound can be acquired because of certain general principles that we develop through analogies. Without this generalization we will not be able to read new words at all. English has several regular words but a great many irregular ones too and, therefore, analogies do not work very well when speaking what foreigners consider a nonphonetic language. Some examples of words that cannot be pronounced analogically are *bead* and *dead*, *put* compared with *but*, and *tough* and *though*. The same pattern of letters has a completely different pronunciation.

4. So, how is it that children can read made-up words? They must be engaged in analogical mechanisms. In languages that are significantly more phonetic than English, such as the languages of Spain and Italy, which are close to Latin, or the languages of India, new words are pronounced successfully

by using the principles of phonological coding. This is because spelling-to-sound relation is, almost always, regular in these languages. Someone with dyslexia in the phonetically regular languages would have difficulty in sound blending (for example, *con-ver-sa-tion*) and may be identified as an unusually slow reader.

5. We must remember that phonological awareness increases as children begin to receive formal instruction. And yet, even before children go to school, the pre-reader is able to do a number of phonological tasks, such as elimination or addition of phonemes, surprisingly well. Research in this area supports the notion that children acquire phonological awareness long before learning to read. The experiences that children have when they are learning rhymes do play an important part in their growing awareness that words and syllables can be made into smaller units of sound. Although we know that teaching rhyme prepares children to read, when combined with spelling, it has the best effect on enhancing reading ability.

There are Many Kinds of Reading Disabilities

What are the different skills that we require for reading? Clearly, the major one is to translate spelling to sound, the phonological coding skill. Given a meaningless word, why does it take longer to read than a real word? Is it because searching for and not finding the word's meaning takes more time? This is certainly a very likely explanation and we can argue that the ultimate purpose of reading is not simply pronouncing what is written, but to understand its meaning.

Some words can be read faster when placed in a meaningful context such as in the sentence *John hit Jack on the nose and Jack was really hurt!* A child may read the word *hurt* faster in this sentence than as a single isolated word in a reading test. However, if the child cannot do phonological coding, that is, has not learnt to associate the letters h-u-r-t with sounds and put these together to sound out the word, he/she will probably read the word as *angry*. Thus, a meaningful context can help phonological coding of a word but children cannot be taught to read a new or strange word (such as *banyan*, *magnolia*) simply by guessing its meaning in a sentence.

So, what we say about the relation between phonological coding and comprehension is simply this: words that have meaning are easier to read and we can read them faster; reading also becomes more interesting if children understand fully what they are given to read. Ask them to read something that they do not understand and they are easily turned off, complaining that it is difficult to read even though they can "sound out" every word perfectly well. We must make sure that children are given words to read in a passage that they can understand. In the chapter on comprehension, we discuss how meaning is derived from what is read or what is spoken.

Difficulties in reading can be caused by many conditions outside reading ability, such as poor motivation or not being exposed to a literate environment at home and in the community. As far as the reading process is concerned, we can conclude the following:

1. The reading problems of some children can be caused by difficulties in comprehension.
2. A slow rate of reading is a sign of reading difficulty, especially when children can code phonologically but have a slow reading speed. In phonetically regular languages such as German, Spanish, and Portuguese, or the classical languages like Latin and Sanskrit, any new word can be read but the speed of reading is unusually slow among dyslexics.
3. A child's word-decoding and comprehension skills are distinct abilities and should be tested separately.

Summing Up

There is, undoubtedly, a need for phonological coding in order to learn to read. The learning of rhymes and alliterations that occurs spontaneously during childhood prepares the child for reading and spelling. However, what seems to be a good predictor of reading is phonemic awareness, that is, the child's ability to break words down into phonemes, to manipulate beginning and end sounds, and to be able to say the sounds when some phonemes are eliminated. As we will discuss in later chapters, short-term memory plays an important part in remembering the sequence of sounds that make up words. At this point it is useful to reiterate the distinction between reading words by themselves and comprehension. The two are quite distinct and engage different psychological processes. While comprehension requires world knowledge, decoding words and identifying them does not require the same type of knowledge or experience that informs the child with regard to societal ideas and events. We will discuss comprehension in subsequent chapters.

3

Stages of Reading Development

There is no doubt that reading is a very complex process. Although it is generally not recognized as a complex system of tasks, it is so for a child learning to read. Anyone with a child who appears to be intelligent, but fails to learn to read, will immediately understand just how complex reading skills are. While speaking is natural and spontaneous, reading has to be taught. Children may learn to read through instruction or by imitating and modeling after family members—older brothers, sisters, aunts, and others. In a literate community, the children are exposed to reading long before they are able to read. We know that the right kind of atmosphere or ambience for reading is provided by older brothers and sisters who are already reading at home.

Magical Marks on Paper

Preschoolers who are not yet reading are frequently noticed to go through a series of developmental stages related to literacy. First of all, we have to remember that, for most children, reading and writing go together, that is, as children begin to read they are also writing.

Just below the level of acquiring reading ability, children often consider any kind of mark made by a pen as equivalent to a word or a sentence. This is the *magical* or the *symbolic stage*. In this stage there is no real connection between the scribble that a child makes and the words the scribble is supposed to represent. "I can write *dog*," the child says, and then scribbles something that bears no similarity to a letter or a word.

The next stage is known as the *pictorial* or *words-as-pictures stage*. As the child gets older and reaches the preschool level, he/she suddenly realizes that words can be read like pictures. Children can recognize and describe pictures at an early age and can also recognize simple words from the pattern of letters, but they are still unable to read the word phonologically, that is, they still do not associate the spelling of a word with its pronunciation; they just read it as a whole using "whole word learning." This is the traditional "look and say" method used by teachers with preschoolers and kindergarten children.

Whole word reading is gradually transformed to reading the word by sound rather than by sight, when children acquire an understanding of the connection between letters and sounds (remember the grapheme–phoneme correspondence). In this stage children learn the sounds of letters, and realize that sounds can be combined to form words and determine the pronunciation of the word. When confronted by the printed word, the ability to read it depends on how well a child can engage with what we have described as phonological coding. This is the *alphabetic stage*, that is, when alphabets acquire sounds that are extremely specific to that alphabet. Children must pay attention to the order in which the letters of the alphabet occur in a particular word (such as *Japanese*). If they do not pay attention to the sequence of the letters, they will never spell it correctly. But it is sufficient to say here that phonological coding appears later than reading by sight or pictorial reading. The alphabetic stage starts with the child recognizing the letters, associating the letter with a particular sound, and then combining the letters with their associated sounds into words. Only then is the child able to read the word.

The Alphabetic Stage Develops Layer by Layer

Is the ability to recognize the letters of the alphabet the essence of the alphabetic stage? Letters, sometimes called graphemes, are made-up of different parts or have features that are combined to form individual letters which are then translated into sounds or phonemes. This is the same as learning grapheme-phoneme correspondence. It is a must, and is a natural beginning for the alphabetic stage, but there are several layers of development within this stage.

Consider its two main components—*phoneme identification* and *phoneme manipulation*. A child may recognize that the letter *m* is the same as the sound *mmm*, or the letter *k* is the sound *kah*. But a further development must occur; the beginning reader has to realize that the *mmm* sound is the first sound in the word *mice* and the *kah* sound is the first one in *kind*. Some children may have to be taught this transition from identifying the sound as a single letter to identifying and locating it in a word. Why is this so? Because, when the word *mice* or *kind* is spoken aloud, the sound for *m* or *k* must be perceived in isolation from the whole word. The remedy is to emphasize the sound of the letter: *mmice, kahkahkind*. Some remedial reading programs use this technique (which clever teachers have used all along) to lengthen the sound of the phoneme for better identification.

A beginning reader may recognize the sound of the first letter but fail to recognize the letters in the middle or at the end of the word.

"Spell *kind*," I ask my 6-year-old granddaughter. She starts with "k-i-?" I prompt, "kah-i-nn-d." She says "k-i-n. Is it *d* or *t*?" She is aware of the phonemes but she cannot recognize all of them in a word; she is progressing through the alphabetic stage. Has she learned to manipulate phonemes, the segmenting of a word into phonemes, and the blending of individual phonemes to form a word? I ask her to read the word *bring*. She cannot. I ask her to say the word *bring*. She repeats the word. "Now," I say, "take away the first sound. How will you say the word now?" When she answers "Ring," I know she is on the way to mastering phoneme manipulation.

Blending sounds in a word is a related skill. A child may not be able to utter the sound *bri* when asked to read *bring*, or may not be able to combine the *n* and *g* to form *ng*.

The implications of this discussion for teaching are clear. The teacher (or any person fulfilling the role, such as a family member or friend) must be aware of the distinctions, so that he/she is able to detect where the child may be having difficulty, and emphasize each component of a word when reading.

How the alphabetic stage progresses naturally to the *orthographic stage*—looking at the sequences of letters and learning how to spell and pronounce the word—is discussed in the next section. (One may ask if a bilingual education helps with the recognition of phonemes and phonemic manipulation. It does seem to do that, but only when the child does not have dyslexia or any other obvious reading difficulties.)

Is there a stage beyond the alphabetic stage, beyond the child's ability to recognize the association between letters and words and their specific sounds? The answer seems to be yes, as far as the English language is concerned. This stage is called the *orthographic* stage. The progression from recognizing letters and simple words to their *orthography* occurs normally in most children. Orthography is concerned with how the word is spelled. As mentioned in Chapter 2, the words *bead* and *dead* have similar spellings but quite different sounds because of the way the letters *e* and *a* are combined and pronounced in the two words. Similarly, the words *though* and *tough* have the same spelling at the end but *ough* is pronounced differently in each of these words. Orthography, therefore, relates closely to the ability to spell. Sometimes, however, children may spell poorly but can read without any difficulty.

In summary, children pass through the following stages (see Figure 3.1):

1. The **symbolic stage** where scribbles and lines are made arbitrarily, the child considering the scribbles as standing for words he/she already knows.
2. The **pictorial** stage where the word is recognized as a picture, a pattern of letters without being analyzed as a distinctive series of letters.
3. The **alphabetic stage** where the child realizes that the letters have specific sounds.
4. The **orthographic** stage where, as the child begins to read fluently, he/she is aware of the way letters could be combined and can produce distinct sounds like *tough*, *though*, and *laugh*.

These stages of reading are taken from a popular model suggested by Uta Frith (1986).

Figure 3.1   Developmental Stages of Reading

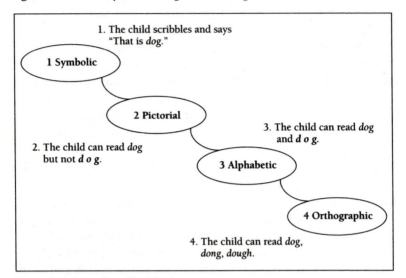

Source: Author, as adapted from Frith.

Note: Children develop reading in stages. First there is the magical stage where any scribble is called a word by the child. In the second stage, the word is read as a picture, so the same word written in a slightly different font is not recognized as the same. The third and most important stage is alphabetic stage where the sequence of the letters is used as a clue to reading the word. Therefore the child can recognize and read the word in any written form. The last stage occurs in nonphonetic languages such as English, when the child becomes aware of possible letter combinations and sounds.

However, the story of progression from the symbolic to the orthographic stage is not universally accepted. As mentioned in Chapter 1, some research has shown that the beginning reader may use both the pictorial representation and the sound representation at the same time, that is, the reader does not have to first read the words as pictures and then move on to reading them as sounds. The two processes may occur simultaneously when some words are recognized as pictures and others are analyzed and read by their sounds. It is also true that orthography may not play an important role in languages such as Spanish, Italian, Sanskrit, and Hindi, where there is a close correspondence between spelling and pronunciation. In these phonetically regular languages, words are most often read as they are spelled.

More about Reading, Speech, and the Brain

The ability to put letters together and sound them out depends on the ability to represent the sounds in one's own internal speech. This is why phonological coding is essentially concerned with how children can represent not only the sounds they hear, but also the sounds as they are associated with letters and words. We are not going to discuss in any detail the various aspects of how children perceive speech, how they do phonological coding, and, ultimately, how they produce spoken responses. These three processes logically follow each other, that is, auditory discrimination of speech, transforming words into sounds, and then producing the speech sounds themselves. Let us simply say that if the child is not able to discriminate between different speech sounds, he/she will have difficulty in representing the sounds in the mind and this will lead to a defective production of spoken words and sentences. These three processes may be quite separate, that is, some children may not be able to perceive speech accurately but can read what is written without much difficulty. Similarly, some children may be able to perceive speech distinctly but may fail to read words or sentences correctly. Finally, a child may be able to do both of these, but may have difficulty in representing them in their minds. The three activities occur in different places in the brain and the neural systems responsible for each activity could be quite distinct from each other. We have some evidence supporting this from studying the speech and reading difficulties of individuals who have suffered damage to different parts of their brains, resulting in very specific language problems.

Dictionaries in the head

We cannot teach children to recognize words only. We expect them to understand what they are reading. Thus, there is a dictionary in our heads for the sound of written letters/words (phonological coding lexicon) and for the meaning of the word (semantic lexicon). Some experts in the field of reading also think of a "pronunciation dictionary". It is not enough that a child can recognize a printed word; he/she must also be able to pronounce it correctly. The pronunciation of the word has to be assembled internally in the child's mind. The next step is for the child to mobilize and organize the word's speech production. Thus the child may have to carry three dictionaries in his head. The first has to do with print-to-sound translation, the second with pronunciation, and the third with the meaning of the word.

Sentences have syntax and meaning

Beyond single words, the child has to read sentences and this is when the third dictionary is often consulted. Also, the reader must have knowledge of the syntax of sentences. The syntax of a sentence and its meaning are like twins—one helps the other. A child can remember the meaning of a sentence by attending to its syntax. At the same time, a child can appreciate the syntax of a sentence better if he/she knows its meaning. What do we mean by appreciation of syntax? Essentially, the reader is required to understand the sequence in which the words occur in a grammatically correct sentence. Sequencing or successive processing, therefore, plays an important part in comprehension of syntax. On the other hand, the semantic aspect or the meaning of a sentence depends upon the way the child puts the ideas in a sentence together. The process of putting together all the ideas in the sentence and seeing their connection to each other requires simultaneous processing. These two processes are dealt with in the next chapter which discusses some of the difficulties encountered in reading development.

Brain activities are responses that accompany reading and speech

The neuropsychological picture of reading concerns the location of phonological coding as well as the oral output of a printed word. As far as we know from neuropsychological damage to the brain, there are distinct functional areas that are activated when, for example, an individual is *reading* a word, *listening* to a word, *speaking* a word, and *generating* a word. The area of the brain that is active when an individual is reading a word from print is in the occipital lobe, whereas the area that is strongly activated when a person is listening to a word is in the overlapping regions of the parietal and temporal lobes. This does not mean that no other area is active when a person is reading a word from print or listening to a word. The brain activities seen in a Positron Emission Tomography (PET) scan overlap to some extent. However, the areas mentioned are maximally activated while reading a word from print as compared to listening to a spoken word. Similarly, when saying a word, the area that is predominately active is close to the front part of the brain. Finally, the front part of the frontal lobe is the region of the brain that shows the most activity when a person is asked to generate words, such as when asked to say as many words as they can that end with the letter. These activities are recorded by PET and help us to understand the process of speech perception and speech production (see Figure 3.2). Therefore, when there is a breakdown in the ability to read, we can analyze the difficulty in terms of these

Figure 3.2   PET Scans of the Brain during Reading Activities

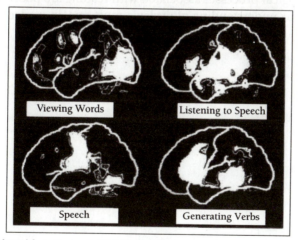

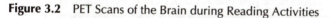

Source: Adapted from Posner and Raichle (1994).

Note: This PET scan picture shows that distinct areas of the brain become active when seeing a printed word, listening to the word spoken, speaking any word, and, finally, making up only one category of words such as verbs. Therefore, word reading difficulties or speech production difficulties can be located in very different parts of the brain.

four different functions. For example, when we wish to distinguish between different kinds of dyslexia or deficit in using words, we might ask whether the child has the same difficulty in listening to words and then reproducing them as he or she has in reading the word. It is possible that a child who has difficulty in reading the word can, nevertheless, listen to and reproduce the word without effort and vice versa.

If a child is unable to say the word or words, that is, cannot repeat spoken words, we must further examine the child to find out if the difficulty in speaking a word is related to words that he has listened to, or words that he has read, or to neither of these. Rather, the child's difficulty may be detected in producing speech. Similarly, if the child has difficulty in generating words we must ask whether this difficulty is associated with or quite distinct from dyslexia.

We believe that there are many kinds of dyslexia, but neuro-psychological evidence now supports four distinct kinds of difficulties relating to words. It is, therefore, too simplistic to believe that poor readers have just one kind of deficit. As long as the neuro-psychological processes associated with reading are poorly understood, our understanding of dyslexia must remain inadequate.

4

Explaining Reading by Intelligence

There are many children who are intelligent but cannot read. We identify some of them as having dyslexia. Indeed, IQ, the popular indication of intelligence, does not predict dyslexia. Many children at all levels of IQ fail to learn to read adequately in spite of getting the same instruction in the classroom as their classmates. That some children with a normal IQ of 100 or better do not learn to read is evidence enough for saying that IQ is not very relevant when explaining or predicting reading disability. In fact, if we agree with this simple and rather obvious statement, we will go against the practices of hundreds of schools in USA and Canada who receive funding for reading-disabled children. This funding is based on the discrepancy between the IQ and reading ability of children on the grounds that the child's IQ would predict a reading level that is significantly higher than his/her actual level of reading.

What is wrong with using this discrepancy between IQ and reading as a basis for deciding which child is reading normally and which one has a learning disability? The truth is, as mentioned above, reading disability is found at all levels of IQ. A child with an IQ of 80 is as likely to show up in a reading disability class or clinic as a child whose IQ is 120. The "discrepancy" notion is wrong from another point of view—it assumes that IQ should predict reading when we might just as well assume the opposite, that reading should predict IQ.

IQ tests, such as the Wechsler Intelligence Scale for Children (WISC), are generally used to predict reading. This is so because many of its test items are included in the school curriculum. Therefore, a child who is learning-disabled and is doing poorly in school is likely to do poorly in the IQ test as well. So the chances of predicting reading or learning ability from IQ tests are as good as its reverse.

What is Intelligence All About?

Is intelligence a general mental ability? The British psychologist Spearman attempted to show that intelligence is general; Cyril Burt (who was greatly influenced by Spearman), and, more recently, Eysenck and Jensen, have all supported the view that there is a common trait of intelligence which runs across much of a person's behavior. They call this the general or g *factor*. Thus, if you agree with Spearman, Burt, Eysenck, and Jensen, you believe that foolishness or intelligence can be general traits of the people we know.

However, all of us know that some people have special abilities. A great vocal musician may not be very good at some other skill. (In fact, individuals who are musically gifted are quite different from those who are generally gifted, that is, those with a high level of intelligence.) What can we conclude, then, about general intelligence? It is safe to assume that most people can be graded on a scale of general intelligence from extremely unintelligent to quite bright. However, there are specific skills, for example, the ability to excel in art, music, mathematics, and writing creative literature, which go against the g factor.

Another characteristic of intelligence that psychologists often mention is that it has to do with knowing, cognition, understanding, and thinking. In other words, intelligence is a cognitive activity, as distinct from an affective activity. If we divide human activities into three forms, namely, thinking, feeling, and willing, intelligence would be most closely related to thinking. Therefore, intelligent behavior would include all forms of cognitive behavior such as perceiving, attending, learning, memorizing, and thinking.

What can we say, then, about intelligence being a cognitive activity? Intelligent behavior is certainly identified with the acquisition of knowledge and with actions which are based on our plans and judgments, but at the same time it is intimately connected with our emotions and feelings. Complex human characteristics such as intelligence are determined not by a single gene but by a number of genes arranged in a particular manner. Therefore, it is very difficult to predict whether or not the child of very intelligent parents will also be highly intelligent. In fact, there is no one-to-one relationship between psychological characteristics and physical characteristics that are inherited through specific genes. The inheritance of intelligence is much more complex and can be proved only in studies that include a large group of people rather than one pair of parents.

Also to be remembered here is the fact that if a characteristic is determined by several millions of genes rather than through one gene, then it is much more open to environmental influences. It is not enough to be born an intelligent baby; unless the baby is given a chance to have a normal life with good nutrition, good medical care, stimulation at home (people talking to the baby), and, later on, opportunity for good education, the child may not grow up to be an intelligent person. In fact, millions of children in the world do not get the opportunity to develop their intelligence; millions do not get a chance for education. Who knows how many of them, given adequate healthcare and a chance for good education, would turn out to be talented artists and leading scientists.

How to Measure Intelligence: American IQ Tests

Intelligence can be measured by tests. At the beginning of this century in Paris, Alfred Binet developed the first set of such tests to find out which children in school needed special attention. So, at the beginning, intelligence tests were mainly used to separate the dull children in school from the average or bright children so that they could receive special education; they were not meant to be free of cultural bias or academic content (see Table 4.1).

Intelligence is expressed in terms of IQ. Tests are developed, that indicate what an average child of a certain age can do; for example, what a 5-year-old can answer but a 4-year-old cannot. In other words, intelligence tests give us a norm for each age. A test is first given to hundreds of children in order to select those questions which the majority of children at that age can answer.

Table 4.1   Examples of Items in an IQ Test

Vocabulary

Tell me what YESTERDAY means?	The day before
	A song by the Beatles
Tell me what CONSUME means?	Eat, drink, use up
	Buy, digest
Tell me what SENTENCE means?	A group of words expressing a complete thought
	A line

Similarities

In what way are a dog and a lion alike?	Both are animals
	Both growl
In what way are work and play alike?	Both are activities valued by society
	Both are necessities of life

Information

What is the world's population?
Who wrote Hamlet?

Comprehension

Why does land in the city cost more than land in the country?

Source: Wechsler (1974).

From such norms we may find that a set of questions for 5-year-olds is successfully answered by about 83 percent of children. These 83 in 100 children have average or above average intelligence. Of the remaining 17 percent of children, only about 3 percent do extremely poorly in the tests and are called mentally retarded children. The remaining 14 percent are sometimes called dull normal children. There is a graph which helps us understand the distribution of intelligence in a normal population.

Some of the questions in an intelligence test are verbal and they require oral or written responses. For example, a question in the verbal form is, "Apples are to oranges as tables are to ... ?" The answer is any item in the furniture category, such as a chair, because apples and oranges belong to the category of fruit. Similarly, "Tall is to short, as up is to ... ?" Another example would be to give the missing number in the series 4, 9, 19, 39....

A variety of questions are used in all standardized intelligence tests. All of them give age norms. If a 5-year-old child passes the tests that average children of the same age can pass, then his mental age is 5. On the other hand, if a 5-year-old child can only pass the test for age 3, then his mental age is 3. The IQ is calculated by dividing the mental age (MA) by the chronological age (CA) and multiplying the answer by 100. Thus in the first case the child has an IQ of 100 $[(5 \div 5) \times 100]$ and in the second case an IQ of 60 $[(3 \div 5) \times 100]$. Therefore, IQ by definition is a measure of how well a child has done in the intelligence test compared to children of similar age. Nearly 67 percent of individuals have an IQ between 85 and 115. Those with IQs of 70 or below are considered to be mentally retarded and constitute some 3 percent of the population. Sometimes, we can understand the level at which a retarded or nonretarded child is functioning by referring to his or her mental age. Suppose we wish to place a retarded boy in a class with normal children, at what academic level should we place him? If his mental age is 7, he would be expected to do most of the class work for 7-year-olds in the school and he could be placed in class 3 or 4. He may, however, have a chronological age of 10.

As you probably know, physical and mental maturation cease in most children at the age of around sixteen. After this age an individual may gain knowledge and experience but, as far as his mental ability is concerned, he can learn whatever a 20-year-old can learn, given the same amount of training. Therefore, the highest mental age that a person can obtain in an intelligence test is 16. (There are, of course, intelligence tests designed for college students and adults who are superior in intelligence. Therefore, if you wish to choose a group of highly intelligent students for an introductory course in a new field, such as how to track satellites, you may give the candidates an intelligence test for superior adults, along with a test of appropriate background knowledge.)

IQ Tests: Some Criticism

Testing intelligence by standard tests has come under attack in the last 15 years. At least three criticisms of intelligence testing have been voiced. First, intelligence tests measure ability and give us an IQ score, but do not show the processes of thinking which determine that ability. Intelligence tests consist of problems to be solved and different persons may solve them by using different processes. One procedure of solving the problem ends in success, another procedure ends in failure. It is important to know why a person failed the test and what processes were not used, rather than the information that the person has failed. Specifically, in the case of children's intelligence testing, teachers or parents do not know why the child did poorly in the test and what processes the child did or did not use. It does not help a teacher to know that two children in the class have the same intelligence but one has great difficulty in reading the text and understanding it, whereas the other has no such problem. So the teacher asks— 'Can I use the information about the children's IQ in order to help the child with reading difficulties?' No, the teacher cannot.

The second criticism of intelligence testing is that the tests require a knowledge of school subjects—those who are in poor schools have a poor education and hence do poorly in the tests. Many people criticize intelligence tests because they measure academic intelligence, not the kind of intelligence that is required if one is to succeed outside school. This is mentioned in the next section of the chapter. So the intelligence tests have limited usefulness.

Third, the tests discriminate against disadvantaged children. Many of the test items can be best answered by children of middle-class and urban families because these children are most familiar with the items. For example, a test question is: "Divide the following into two groups: mango, potato, cauliflower, orange, grape." A middle-class child is perhaps more familiar with all of these and their use than a lower-class child, thus the former has no problem in separating the words into 'fruits' and 'vegetables'. The criticism, then, is that standard intelligence tests are biased in favor of the middle-class urban culture. Social disadvantage undoubtedly lowers intelligence scores of children (Das, 1998: 217–18).

The PASS Theory of Intelligence: An Alternative to IQ

The PASS (Planning, Arousal-Attention, Simultaneous, Successive) cognitive processing model can be described as a modern theory.

It is concerned with information processing that is dynamic as opposed to static. It is based on Luria's analyses of brain structures (Luria, 1966b, 1973). Luria was a Russian neuropsychologist and medical doctor who examined many patients suffering from brain damage. He worked for 50 years in this field and died in 1977.

Luria described human cognitive processes within the framework of three functional units. The function of the first unit is cortical arousal and attention; the second unit codes information using simultaneous and successive processes; the third unit provides for planning, self-monitoring, and structuring of cognitive activities. Luria's work on the functional aspects of brain structures formed the basis of the PASS model.

The PASS theory, shown in Figure 4.1, provides a model for conceptualizing human intellectual competence. The rationale for test construction is derived from the theory. We get information or input through our eyes, ears, nose, skin, tongue, and internal organs. When the sensory information is sent for analysis, the central processes become active. There are four components that make up the central processing mechanisms and together they make up PASS:

1. Planning (P)
2. Arousal-Attention (A)
3. Simultaneous Processing (S)
4. Successive Processing (S)

An important addition is *knowledge-base*. This is made up of past experiences and learning, and of emotions and motivations that provide the background for information to be processed. The four processes must be active in the context of an individual's knowledge-base. It is as if PASS processes are floating on a sea of knowledge; without the water they cannot operate and will sink. For example, if a child does not know the letters of the alphabet he cannot process the letters serially and read a word like *going*. If the child does not understand the words, he cannot process the meaning of a sentence by putting the ideas together simultaneously, as in "My dog bit my cat." He will not be able to answer the question, "Who was hurt?" (Answer—my cat).

Figure 4.1   The PASS Model

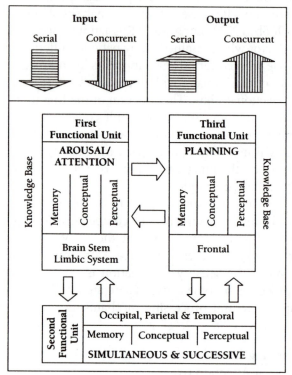

Source: Adapted from Naglieri (1999).
Note: The diagram shows the components of input, knowledge base, the processes of arousal, planning, simultaneous-successive information coding, and, finally, output.

The four major processes are associated with different parts of the brain. *Planning* is broadly located in the front part of our brains, the frontal lobe. We give a special place to planning in our mental activities. Planning processes will be required when the individual makes decisions about how to solve a problem or carry out an activity, how to write an essay about the last summer vacation, or what to say to a friend who has lost his father. Planning is also needed to focus our attention and to decide how and when to use simultaneous and successive processes. For example, writing a composition or a story involves the generation of a plan, the organization of ideas, control over what is presented when, examination of the product, and revisions to ensure a good final product.

Arousal-Attention is more difficult to locate. Arousal is a simple process that keeps us awake and alert and is associated with the activities in the brain stem and the lower part of the cerebral cortex. Attention is more complex and just as we can get alerted by things that interest us, we can fall asleep during a boring lecture or conversation. What part of the brain decides whether or not something that we are experiencing is interesting? Perhaps the frontal lobe and the lower parts of the cortex together do this.

Simultaneous Processing and *Successive Processing* are located in the back part of the brain. Simultaneous processing is broadly associated with the occipital and the parietal lobes whereas successive processing is associated with the frontotemporal lobe.

The last component of the PASS model is *Output* or action and behavior. If you ask a child to memorize, word by word, the definition of democracy from his text book in social studies, he must use a strictly successive process. But if you ask him to describe what democracy is all about, he could use simultaneous processing, putting the main ideas about democracy together and telling you the answer. A child who fails in the first task may be successful in the second. Therefore, just by changing the nature of the answer (output), we can change the processing required to arrive at that answer.

Some people who have lost their memory as a result of a brain disease can nevertheless recall it with a little prompting. Therefore, how we measure output becomes important in measuring intelligence. The PASS theory of intelligence has given us:

- **Tests** to measure intelligence as a set of cognitive processes;
- **Discussion** about what the major processes are;
- **Guidance** for remediation of the processing difficulties that an individual might have.

Collaboratively, they introduce advantages over old measures of IQ.

Why IQ may Predict Reading Ability

Why then is IQ widely believed to predict reading ability? Is it because IQ measures potential whereas reading ability is an achievement? It is argued that IQ, as potential, should be manifested or expressed in reading as in other behavior. But, let us note from the example of Wechsler testing that some test items are in fact tests of vocabulary and arithmetic, which are subjects taught in the schools. Even tests of general information are taught in social studies. It is not surprising, then, that we can predict from the IQ score of a child his/her reading, arithmetic, or general learning ability, and that we can reverse the prediction as well.

So IQ may be irrelevant in the diagnosis of reading disability but it may predict reading ability. These predictions can be made mainly because the IQ tests contain questions that are based on school subjects. But is intellectual ability or intelligence in a broad sense, not in the narrow sense of IQ tests, irrelevant for the understanding and prediction of reading disability? It is obviously not so, because we suspect that reading depends on basic intellectual processes as suggested in the previous chapters. We shall discuss this in some detail here.

IQ is Irrelevant but Cognitive Processes are Relevant

What other processes may be critical for word reading besides phonological coding? According to some researchers, phonological skills may not tell the whole story because deficient phonological skills are themselves an outcome of difficulties experienced with more fundamental cognitive processes. Indeed, it has been suggested that one cognitive aspect—*working memory*—is directly related to reading together with phonological processing and syntactic awareness. (*Dog bites man* and *Man bites dog* do not differ in syntax but they are different in meaning.)

Working memory is simply like a desktop computer that has the capacity to remember input for short periods of time (RAM). This analogy applies to the limited period of time the child has when working with recently learnt material. For example, if one says to a child, "The blue yellowed the pin" and then asks who was yellowed, the child has to hold the content of the sentence in his/her mind long enough to work out the solution. The child keeps the sentence alive in memory by rehearsing it. This is often done automatically and the child is not even aware of it.

The sentence can also be said to go through an articulation loop. While working memory, and particularly the articulatory (phonological) loop, certainly seems to play a role in reading difficulties, its influence may be too broadly interpreted. For example, not all reading-disabled children exhibit working memory problems. Also, how the development of working memory is specifically connected to reading acquisition is not fully understood or explained. In the light of these shortcomings, we believe that the search for relevant cognitive processes needs simultaneously to include and go beyond working memory.

Our search has led to processes other than phonological ones and answers the question: "Why do some children fail to acquire the necessary phonological coding skills in the first place?" We have proposed that PASS can help explain reading and reading disability.

However, no task requires solely simultaneous or successive processing; it is a matter of emphasis. For example, word reading can involve an interplay of simultaneous and successive processing, letter recognition predominantly involves simultaneous processing, detecting their serial order in a syllable requires successive processing, combining the syllables requires simultaneous processing, and so on. Due to the importance of phonological coding in the early stages of word reading, successive processing is naturally expected to be more important at this level. Simultaneous processing, in turn, should be more strongly related to reading comprehension than to word decoding. In reading comprehension, simultaneous processing is needed to interrelate meaningful units and integrating them into higher-level units. Planning and attention are necessary at all levels of reading, although common decoding tasks are not likely to be affected by minor differences in these executive processes. However, their importance should rise as a function of task complexity.

We conclude that two types of cognitive processes are necessary for reading acquisition: (a) those that contribute to the development of phonological processing, in particular, and to encoding of print, in general, such as successive and simultaneous processing; and (b) those, such as attention and planning, that allow the successful deployment of phonological and other skills.

Examples of PASS Tasks from the Das-Naglieri Assessment System

Arousal-attention tasks

Three tasks are given to find out about children's processing in each of the four PASS processes. Thus, there are three tasks to measure arousal-attention. One of these, a task for receptive attention, is given in Figure 4.2 as an example. Each item in this task consists of a pair of letters. The child is asked to underline the pair that has the same letter in capital and in lowercase. Some pairs have different letters; these are the distractions that the child must avoid and they should not be underlined.

Figure 4.2   A Task for Assessing Receptive Attention

EB **bB**	nh	RA	eR	nA	rR	An	**AA**
eE bN	rR	eT	Tb	**EN**	bT	eE	**nE**

Source: Author.

The simultaneous processing tasks

Simultaneous processing is measured by three tests. One of these is Verbal Spatial Relations. This test requires the child to understand logical and grammatical relations, such as a triangle within a circle that is within a square. The examiner reads each question at the bottom of the pictures, for example: Which picture shows a square to the left of a circle that is under a triangle? The child is asked to point to the correct picture as quickly as possible (see Figure 4.3).

Tests of planning

Planning subtests require the child to develop a plan of action, evaluate the value of the method, monitor its effectiveness, revise or reject a previous plan as the task demands change, and control the impulse to act without careful consideration. Planning is central to

Figure 4.3   Tasks for Assessing Simultaneous Processing

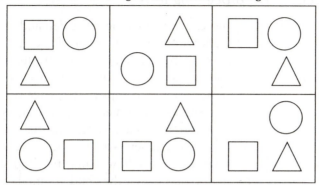

Source: Author.

all activities in which there is both intentionality and a need for some method to solve a problem. This process includes self-monitoring and impulse control as well as plan generation.

Planning as a process that demands the development and use of strategies to solve problems is well illustrated by the Planned Codes test (see Figure 4.4). This test requires the child to write a code (for example, OO or XO) under the corresponding letter (for example, A or B).Children can use different strategies to complete the test in an efficient and timely manner (Adapted from Naglieri, 1999).

Figure 4.4   Example of a Planning Test Item

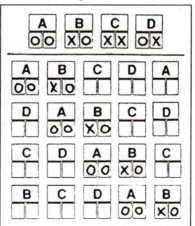

Source: Author.

The successive processing tests

A test that involves successive processing must demand that the child attend to and work with the linear order of events. This is most easily evaluated by the subtest Word Series. In this subtest the child simply repeats words in the exact order in which they are stated by the examiner. A more complex successive subtest is Sentence Questions. This subtest, illustrated in Figure 4.5, requires the child to answer a question about a statement made by the examiner. For example, the examiner says, "The red greened the blue with a yellow. Who used the yellow?" and the child should say, "The red." This item requires that the child comprehend the sequence of words to arrive at the correct solution, making it an excellent measure of successive processing (adapted from Naglieri, 1999: 12–13).

Figure 4.5   Example of a Successive Processing Test Item

> 1. The blue is yellow. Who is yellow?
>
> 2. The red greened the blue with a yellow. Who used the yellow?
>
> 3. The red blues a yellow green of pinks, that are brown in the purple, and then greys the tan. What does the red do first?

Source: Author.

A Look at Types of Reading Disabilities: Division by Cognitive Processes?

Many of us would ask whether we can find different types of children with reading disability. If we can, it will clean up the heterogeneous mess and allow us to understand the reading-disabled children's difficulties in terms of the cognitive processing mode they use. For example, who belongs to the true dyslexic category? Who should we place in the so-called garden-variety category? Does everyone who has reading difficulties also show a distinct pattern of deficits in cognitive processing? What is the value of classification or subtyping in terms of cognitive processes?

There has been recent research to identify the subtypes. We mention two studies, one done by our team of researchers at the Developmental Disabilities Centre and the other by Morris and colleagues (1998), a group of scientists in USA.

In our own research we conducted the PASS tests as well as tests of reading ability. Our sample was made up of 65 children in Grade 2 classes. Their performance on the reading tests had shown a very poor level of reading competence for single words and nonwords (for example, *fiba*, *brampt*). We grouped their scores into clusters by cluster analysis, which is a statistical procedure. Three clusters of children emerged: first, a group which had poor scores in almost all of our PASS processes; second, a group with poor scores mainly on successive processes; and third, a very small group of only nine children who were *not* poor performers in the PASS tests, but were reading poorly. We had, thus, found the garden variety (first group), the dyslexic (second group) and the 'no-deficit' group (the third group).

Thus, the PASS theory is useful for resolving the confusion and also for guiding the educator who has to deal with the heterogeneous class of reading-disabled children. The study suggests that guidance for managing instruction, according to the strength and weakness in the child's cognitive functions, can be provided.

A recent study in USA that tried to classify reading disabilities used many tests that, while not taken directly from the PASS tests, were very similar. The focus of this study was to discriminate between different types of reading-disabled children within a heterogeneous group of 232 children made up of both good and poor readers. The scientists in this study also used cluster analysis to look at subtypes. Seven reading-disabled subtypes emerged and two were normal readers. The authors used cognitive tests, linguistic and neuropsychological tests, and tests of phonological coding and reading. The tests that were found to be important for subtyping were tests of phonological awareness, word recall (successive tests), rapid naming (successive), similarities (simultaneous), speed of articulation (successive), judgment of line orientation and visual–spatial judgment (simultaneous), visual attention (attention), and nonverbal short-term memory (successive). Thus, looking at the tests that were used, one could easily put them into the PASS category of tests and, although the authors (Morris et al., 1998) did not use the PASS theory in explaining their results, it is clear that PASS processes are extremely relevant here to understand the clusters that emerged.

In previous chapters we discussed how the two major difficulties of reading-disabled children were word decoding and phonological awareness. We add the selected PASS processes to this list. Difficulties in successive processing are typically found among beginning readers, who are likely to be dyslexics, whereas most general poor readers may be weak to a certain extent in all the PASS processes. However, in spite of intact PASS processes normal for their age, some children still do not learn to read adequately.

Children who are experiencing reading difficulties may primarily have a problem in their successive and simultaneous processing, when all other noncognitive causes are ruled out. The noncognitive causes can include poor instruction, lack of motivation, cultural disadvantage, malnutrition, and several kinds of physical and sensory handicaps—deafness, cerebral palsy, and so on. The PASS processes in which a child may be weak must be determined; this helps us to choose an appropriate program for remediation, as described in the last three chapters of the book (Part II). Reading may be poor in children who have a problem in arousal-attention. Once that condition is controlled (for example, by drugs or behavioral programs), then the child's reading ability may improve. Some children may be clumsy and disorganized, probably due to a deficit in their planning process. Again, if that is their primary processing difficulty, an appropriate program must be designed to help such children. A classic dyslexic usually has poor successive processing, while all other processes are adequate. Thus, a PASS profile of the child is useful in individualized planning programs.

Summing Up

We hope that a clear theory of the processes required for reading has been presented in this and the previous chapters. If so, word-reading disability should have been understood. The questions still to be answered are: "Can we help prevent reading disability?" and "Can we remediate reading disability?" We discuss these in subsequent chapters. However, reading also requires comprehension. Furthermore, spelling and writing go hand in hand with reading. The next two chapters discuss this relationship.

5

Reading and Comprehension

How do We Understand What We Understand?

It took reading specialists many years to realize that understanding what you read and reading itself require two different processes. There are children who can read but cannot understand, and there are children who cannot read well because of some problem with speech but who, nevertheless, can understand through silent reading.

Reading involves decoding words and identifying the sound that must accompany the printed word. Reading as word decoding is used in the translation of spelling to speech. So, do the two aspects of reading require some abilities that are common? Does understanding what we read involve some abilities similar to those required when reading words?

What is Involved in Comprehension?

One of the first things to understand is the difference between reading comprehension and listening comprehension. The processes for the two are essentially the same, but the manner in which we get the input is different. Obviously, the child does not need to read if we want him/her to understand oral presentations. The child does not have to decode words or bother learning the phonological characteristics of printed words if he/she is listening to speech. Thus, many children who have comprehension problems can be helped if we record what is written in a passage or a story on a tape recorder and play it back to them. If they have no difficulty in comprehension after listening to the tape recording, then they really do not have a problem in comprehension.

It is also clear that if some children have a great difficulty in reading—reading slowly or with hesitation—then their comprehension is threatened because a great deal of resources or capacity is taken up by the activity of reading itself. Therefore, children who are slow readers and who read each word with difficulty may be wrongly diagnosed as having comprehension difficulties. Clearly, we should give all children who are experiencing comprehension problems, both listening and reading comprehension tasks.

Having said that, we must consider that in presenting oral speech, the child (or even the adult) has a different problem in comprehension, compared to the presentation of the material in written form. In the oral form, the individual cannot go back to what he/she has heard unless it is a mechanical presentation through a tape recorder. To understand, a listener will require intellectual processes such as attention, specifically attention to the sequence of speech. For example, if a speaker is presenting a long sentence such as *The house that Jack built was burned by an arsonist named Jim*, and the listener is asked who burned the house, attention must be paid to the sequence in which the words occur. This is similar to reading comprehension in that the reader is required to pay attention to and analyze the sequence of the words in a sentence. The difference is that the reader can go back and read the sentence over and over again until the meaning becomes clear, whereas in the case of a listener this is not possible.

Another point that becomes clear with regard to comprehension is syntax. Material that is presented verbally is usually adjusted to the listener's limited capacity for processing very long sentences. A good speaker is naturally aware of the listener's needs and adjusts the structure of sentences and paragraphs accordingly. However, in written material, the writer has some freedom to use relatively complex syntax than a speaker might use, while remaining aware of the reader's needs with regard to putting things in context and giving the reader cues to anticipate how the paragraph or the discourse is going to end.

First Analyze Words and Syntax, then Understand

Both listening and reading are involved in comprehension and are further summarized here. Reading may involve single words while comprehension usually involves a sentence, a paragraph, or an entire discourse. When we read, one of the first things we do is analyze the sequence of words in a phrase or sentence. The most commonly occurring phrases are noun phrases or verb phrases. An example of each might be:

> Sentence: *She liked the dog*
> Noun phrase: She
> Verb phrase: ... liked the dog (verb: liked)
> Noun phrase: ... the dog

Let us take another sentence: *Jim was sad as he walked down the garden path in winter*. This sentence contains a noun phrase, a verb phrase, and another noun phrase. When we read a passage, we break it down into meaningful sections—phrases, clauses, and sentences—and analyze these one after another to extract their meaning. As we proceed, we relate the meaning of each successive phrase to that of the preceding one and in this way build our understanding, until at the end we are able to comprehend the whole. We do this quickly, automatically, and with little conscious effort or thought, unless the passage is very complicated. This kind of analysis of syntax, (that is, the grammatical arrangement of words in a sentence) is called *parsing* and is essential for comprehension.

While speaking or reading, we usually stop at the end of a phrase or a clause. (A humorous riddle to illustrate this: What's the difference between a cat and a sentence? Answer: A cat has claws at the end of its paws; a sentence has a pause at the end of its clause.) Do we read sentences phrase by phrase or clause by clause? The answer is—in phrases. Dividing sentences into phrases helps us to divide the sentence into meaningful parts, which we remember while processing its meaning. Thus, while understanding a sentence, we (*a*) try to get as much meaning as possible from the words in a phrase; (*b*) understand the phrase; (*c*) make bridges between the phrases, and, finally, (*d*) spend some time putting it all together at the end of a sentence.

We also pick up cues or signs from the order of words. In the two sentences, *Dog bites man* and *Man bites dog,* there are no changes except in the order of the words, yet the meaning is very different. On the other hand, the order of words and the words themselves may be different, while the meaning remains the same. For example: *I took a bath before dinner* and *Before dinner I took a bath.* The word order is different but the reader derives the same meaning. In a truly ambiguous sentence the meaning depends on the context or the mental set of the person, as the words remain the same. Consider the sentence, *The fat man doesn't take his daily meal.* The listener wonders, "How could he be overweight then? He must be eating at night." For an example of a sentence where the context takes on an important role, consider the following advertisement: "If your wife is not happy in The Baker's Arms, The Feathers may tickle her fancy." Underneath is the sign of a pub named The Feathers and the sign of a particular brand of beer.

Another important cue or sign that helps us understand syntax is word class. A word may be a noun, an adjective, an adverb, a verb, and so on, and it is important that we understand which class it is. An example makes it clear: *my husband was happy* compared to *my happy husband.* Using the two different parts of the sentence, I could say *my husband was happy to see a clean oven* or *my happy husband cleaned the oven.* Here are some other interesting examples: *visiting relatives can be boring; flying planes can be dangerous.* In these examples the clues for understanding the sentence are provided by the word class. The sentence *visiting relatives can be boring* can be interpreted in two ways: either the relatives who are visiting can be boring or one could be bored while visiting relatives.

Words may also be conjunctions, articles or prepositions, such as *the, and, of.* These are also known as the function words. They tell the reader or the listener about the syntax or the meaning of the sentence rather than the content. Consider the following sentence: *I told her baby stories.* It could mean that I told stories to her baby or that I was telling stories meant for babies. So there is a need to include something that resolves the ambiguity. The next sentence, *I fed her dog biscuits,* is altered in meaning according to where the word *the* is inserted: *I fed her the dog biscuits* or *I fed the dog her biscuits.*

There are other signs by which we analyze the syntax of a sentence. These are *punctuation,* word *meaning* and *affixes.* It is very easy to understand how punctuation, such as question marks, exclamation marks and quotations, is important, for example, *You lost the bag!* or *You lost the bag?*

Word meaning helps us understand syntax. This is where meaning and syntax interact with each other. Consider the sentence, *I saw the boy pick up a bat after school.* The boy could have picked up a live bat hanging upside down from a tree, but it is more likely that the majority of readers or listeners will understand that the boy picked up a baseball bat to play with. Compare *On a stormy night the car took the right turn and ended up in a ditch* to *On a stormy night the car took the right turn and ended up just in front of his house.*

By attaching the appropriate endings for a verb or an adverb we can usually understand syntax better than when these affixes are missing. Children learn to attach affixes very early as they start talking. Adults seem to understand perfectly what the child means even though the affix might be quite inappropriate: *I goed to school, She was badder today.* However, sometimes affixes do not help, as in *They're shooting stars* or *I married my daughter.* Both of these sentences can only be understood in terms of context. The reason for describing, in such detail, how we break down sentences or analyze them in terms of syntax is to highlight the importance of syntax in comprehension. (For further discussion, refer to Just and Carpenter, 1977 or Harley, 1995.) Comprehension is essentially getting at the meaning of the sentence and syntax helps with this.

Comprehension is Automatic Most of the Time

Another element of understanding or comprehension lies beyond syntax. When I listen to someone talking and I understand what they say, do I go through the different steps of syntax analysis mentioned above? Do I parse the sentence, determine the word class, and analyze punctuation? The answer is yes, but I do it very quickly and automatically without much effort or thinking. I also understand speech and written text by establishing many connections and linking the material to my knowledge.

When asked whether they have understood what has been said, the answer given by some people reveals their knowledge-base, their experiences, and, let us not forget, the feelings and emotions that are aroused by the speech or text. For example, "Our sweetest songs are those that tell of saddest thoughts" invokes my feelings and emotions to complete my understanding of the sentence. The famous opening line of Tolstoy's *Anna Karenina*, "Happy families are all alike; every unhappy family is unhappy in its own way," will strike individuals in different ways according to their own experiences. Thus, there is no doubt that my understanding depends on my past, my history; it is autobiographical.

The comprehension of a school text may depend more on logic and knowledge previously given in textbooks than on autobiographical experience. It is determined more by knowledge gained in school than by feelings and emotions, but even the factual text can stir up emotions that make the material more meaningful. Superficial understanding of a sentence like *I can resist everything except temptation* may not cause amusement in a Grade 4 child who can just understand the words but cannot enjoy the absurdity of the sentence. A child who does not know the economic condition of present-day Russia would not understand the dark humor making the rounds in Moscow—*I got no food and got no one to bury me.*

We learn a great deal through formal instruction, reading books and magazines, watching TV, interacting with others, generating ideas, and also from our own thoughts. Together these make up our world knowledge, the other important ingredient for comprehension that goes beyond our ability to analyze the syntax or the grammar in a statement. It is the knowledge of oneself, of personal history, of our past learning and culture, as well as inferences and reflections. We can teach the rules of syntax to a child whose comprehension is poor, but experience and world knowledge cannot be acquired easily through formal instruction. The role of knowledge and language as cultural products has to be understood if we are to prescribe remediation for poor comprehension.

Thus children's difficulty in comprehension may go beyond syntax. Meaning beyond syntax, as argued earlier, is derived from the cultural context and autobiographical experiences of children as much as from formal education. That is why we need to encourage our own communication with children, to take them out, engage them in casual conversation, and give them the opportunity to model after an adult's socially acceptable behavior. These are just some of the benefits of adult–child interaction. Unfortunately, for many reasons, some children may lack these opportunities for inter-action with responsible and caring adults and it is not hard to under-stand why they will lack comprehension of text and speech.

Meaning and Sense

Understanding a word which is the vital component of a sentence involves both meaning and sense. Vygotsky (1962) discusses this beautifully. A word has a dictionary meaning but can be used in different ways. Its sense is variable whereas its meaning may be stable. *Her first kiss* and *the kiss of death* have clearly different senses that a child in early school years may miss completely. A word is a symbol, like a gesture, and thus its sense is determined in a complex way. Writers of scientific prose try to use the same word in the same sense throughout their texts, whereas in a story or narrative, the writer knowingly plays upon the different senses of the word and this makes for creative writing.

What determines the sense of a sentence? Consider the simple sentence, "You are you, that's why I pay off your debt by loving you for ever!" The words in this sentence have an ordinary meaning, but are used in a special sense. The sense of the sentence varies, de-pending on the community of readers and, in this case, the mean-ing of the words would have different senses for a young child and a young man in love.

Narratives or texts are made from sentences. Here we observe that (*a*) the sense of oral speech or written text may be very much determined by sentences, (*b*) the *theme* or *sense* of a speech, narrative, or text influences the sense of the sentences it contains, and (*c*) the sentence determines the sense of the word. Thus, understanding a discourse can be a top–down process. For example, the meaning and purpose of the following advertisement were certainly lost or, worse, roused annoyance. It was Sunday morning and the church bells were ringing as I switched on my TV for a moment to see the weather. What assailed me was the loud announcement "God saves, but SAFEWAY saves more!" We admit that comprehension is a complex process.

Consider what helps comprehension. First, words have to be understood but a vocabulary alone is not enough. Words reflect the thoughts of the writer and should be questioned: What does the writer wish to convey? In what sense do I understand it, irrespective of the writer's intention? Are the words meaningless and empty of thought? If the words are, in fact, meaningless, they certainly do detract from our understanding or, even worse, as N. Gumilev wrote: "... like bees in a deserted hive, the dead words have a rotten smell" (cited in Vygotsky, 1986: 255).

A second element of comprehension involves parsing—dividing the sentence in specific ways: Is a sentence written in the form subject–object–verb, or as subject–verb–object? Further, what word classes are there? As discussed previously, analysis of syntax is essential but not sufficient for comprehension.

Third, therefore, we should relate speech or writing to our knowledge-base. This part may be the most difficult for remedial reading that aims at improving comprehension. Cultural knowledge of the individual who comprehends is as helpful as correctly attributing intentions to the speaker or the writer; each has an important role. The result is a scenario or schema that is formed as we listen or read. We have to infer the theme of the text, continuously revising our inferences as we read, anticipating, monitoring, and adjusting our schema in a way that will finally lead to comprehension. There is as much of us in our comprehension as of the writer. Comprehension is truly an interactive process.

Good Listening Comprehension but Poor Reading Comprehension

Understanding what was said and what was read are two different mental processes. If some children experience difficulties in reading, is it any wonder that they will have a hard time understanding written text? The same children may have little difficulty understanding what is read or said to them. These children, who have significant problems in reading comprehension but little or no difficulty in listening comprehension, may truly be dyslexic when compared to other children of their class. In fact, the difference between these two abilities is a good measure of reading disability and a more reliable indicator of dyslexia. Compare this method of identifying dyslexia with the IQ–Reading Difference method that shows that a dyslexic child may be poor in reading, in proportion to his/her low IQ. We may be faced with the absurd result of an intelligent (high IQ) child who reads at the same level as his/her classmates being labeled a poor reader. In the previous chapter, we discussed why IQ cannot help us to understand reading disability; now we understand how unhelpful it is in the identification of truly dyslexic children as opposed to the garden-variety poor readers.

The garden-variety poor reader, who is also poor in listening and reading comprehension, may have an inadequate vocabulary, insufficient understanding of the syntax of the sentences, as well as difficulties in more than one cognitive process—simultaneous processing may be particularly poor, but successive and planning processes may not be as good as of a classmate who reads normally.

According to one estimate, 5.1 percent of children are found to have difficulty in both reading and listening comprehension, whereas only 2.7 percent have difficulty only in reading comprehension. Perhaps these are the true dyslexics. Does good listening comprehension ability indicate that the child has a high IQ, and does poor ability predict a low IQ? Generally, this is true to a certain extent. (The correlation between IQ and comprehension can be up to 0.47.)

Is it easier for many of us to understand what is said rather than what is read? Such a comparison can only be made if the learner both listens to and reads the same text. Will the text be easier to understand when it is read aloud to the learner than if the learner reads it to him/herself? This in itself is quite a complex exercise, bearing in mind that reading the text aloud must take the same time as reading it silently. Furthermore, the person who reads it to the learner must use a monotone to avoid adding emphasis and exclamations, because these would bring the text alive and may make it easier to understand.

Text written by creative writers becomes interesting by incorporating the accents and many nuances of the language. By playing on the sense of the words beyond their meaning, writing can compete well with speech. Spelling and writing is the topic of the next chapter that discusses how we should mean what we write and write what we mean, to paraphrase a statement from *Alice in Wonderland.*

Summary of Reading: What do You Do When You See a Word?

Before ending the discussion on comprehension, let us summarize the course of action that a reader takes when given a printed or written word. Two routes can be followed, as discussed in Chapter 1 (see Figure 5.1):

1. If the word is familiar, one that the reader has seen before and knows, then the "visual route" is followed; the reader is likely to read the word as a whole and understand its meaning, although often unaware of the sequence of letters in the word.
2. If the reader sees a less familiar or a new word, he/she must look at the sequence of the letters in it, say the word, and then read it by sounding it out—the "phonological route". The reader reads the word part by part, often as syllables, noting the succession of letters and sounds. Orthography is noticed. While reading fluently it is sometimes unnecessary for the reader to say the word to him/herself.

The interesting question is, when does comprehension of the word occur—before or after sounding it out? Does the reader understand the meaning of the word as soon as the letter sequences are put together and then sound it out? In both cases the word is converted to its sound, which is phonology. If a word is to be read aloud, a pronunciation is assembled and the word is spoken or articulated. Oral production of the word has occurred. The purpose of reading

Figure 5.1   Reading by Sight and Sound

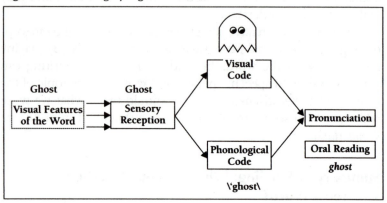

Source: Author.

Note: The word is first seen by our eyes. It has a general shape, like a picture. It has a sequence of letters (G,H,O,S,T in this case). Both of these are seen by the eyes. However, some children read it as a picture with a specific shape, perhaps the same way as they would "read" the picture in the diagram. Other children read the word as a sequence of letters and their sounds, which is reading by phonology. In either case, the word has to be pronounced. Its pronunciation is assembled in the child's head and then an appropriate action plan for speech production, for the tongue, larynx, and so on, is put into action. Sound is now added and we hear the word from the mouth of the reader.

is comprehension; however, these stages leading to comprehension also need to be clearly understood. In a later chapter on PREP, the tasks that promote comprehension are discussed.

6

Spelling and Writing

How do We Learn to Spell?

Some children are taught to spell when they learn to read; for these children, spelling and reading are integrated. Other children are taught to read without ever receiving formal spelling instructions. Whether or not we learn to spell correctly, the fact remains that spelling has to be accurate to convey the meaning of a written word. Just as people who mispronounce words are hard to understand, people who misspell words are hard to understand when their mode of communication is writing. The question, then, is not whether spelling is important but how we learn to spell, and what the relationship between spelling and reading is?

I asked a 5-year-old who is in kindergarten to spell a few words that she already understood. She could orally spell simple words like *mat*, *hat*, *fat*, and even *cat* because she knew that the *c* in cat is said like *k*. However, given words that have a *u* in them, such as *bull*, she checked whether after *b* there was a *u* or an *a*. Similarly, while spelling the word *box*, she asked, "Is it a *b* or an *o*?" This child obviously shows some of the well-known strategies for spelling.

Clearly, (*a*) she knows the sounds of letters, (*b*) she knows that in regular words the middle vowel could have more than one sound, and (*c*) she has little difficulty in tasks that test phonemic awareness. Tasks for phonemic awareness might ask, "In the word *ball*, if you take away the sound *buh*, what will remain?" She says, "All." You may wonder, then, about this girl who already seems to know phonological coding and can do phonological awareness tasks before she enters kindergarten. Can she not simply translate her own speech to letters of the alphabet? How does she answer the above question about the ball? Perhaps she has a good guess about the spelling of the word *ball* and can eliminate the first letter of the word.

How does she spell? She does it in at least two different ways. She could spell some words as a whole; this is called "vocabulary-based spelling". Just as she reads some words as a whole without analyzing the letters or the sounds in the word, she can spell very familiar words such as *cat* without breaking up the word into its component sounds. On the other hand, even for similar words like *hat* and *mat*, she was observed to be using phonological analysis: *huh, huh,* and *muh, muh,* that is, her lips were sounding out the first consonant, followed by the same constellation of vowel and consonant that is common to *cat, mat,* and *hat*. The first consonant is called the "onset", followed by a vowel and consonant constellation called the "rime".

Is Spelling Like Reading? Is Reading Like Spelling?

Are spelling and reading, then, flip sides of a coin? If reading is usually described as translating spelling to speech, spelling could be just the reverse process of translating speech to spelling. To continue the analogy, remember that one of the major activities when children are learning to read consists of grapheme–phoneme correspondence, that is, being able to produce the phonological structure or, in simple words, to recapture the sounds of the printed letters, syllables, or words. Can we then say that spelling is a phoneme-grapheme correspondence? Will common sense support us? The answer is partly yes and partly no.

We should really think of the different strategies that children use in spelling. The pool of knowledge about how anyone spells a word is fed by many streams. For example, when studying patients with brain damage, we can guess not only what part of the brain, when damaged, shows up in what kind of language disorder, but also gain insight into the nature of language-related functions. One of the facts that we learned from a study of patients with brain damage due to a tumor, injury, or deterioration of brain matter was that some patients could not spell a word after they had a brief look at it, while other patients could spell the word when it was written but not when they heard it spoken.

In these findings, we have to remember that when a written word is shown to a patient, or for that matter to a child, the time given for looking at the word is so short that unless they know the spelling of the word, they will not be able to reproduce it in writing. Along with these two groups of patients, there is a third type that may have the added difficulty of putting the letters into a correct sequence to form a word that they already know and are able to read. In these cases, knowing the spelling of a word may not always translate into writing the word correctly.

Are these the types of spelling difficulties we find in normal children or adults? Perhaps the answer is obvious to a parent familiar with the problems her child experiences.

> Yes! I see that in my child who is in Grade 3. She learned to spell some of the words as a whole (a vocabulary-based spelling strategy). At the same time, she also learned how to sound out the letters in the word while spelling. I have also noticed that even when she knew the spelling of a word, when she wrote it down letter by letter, she would make mistakes in the sequence, especially in long words such as *sequence* or *vaccine*. She would do things like omit the last *e*, or make the majority of her sequencing errors in the middle part of a long word.

So, is reading like spelling and spelling like reading? The answer to the above puzzle is once again partly yes and partly no.

Does Spelling Go through Stages?

Spelling does appear to go through the same stages as reading. Furthermore, the issues and controversies that have been raised in trying to understand reading have also been raised in spelling. In the previous chapter, we discussed the different stages of reading, particularly the stages from magical to orthographic as suggested by Uta Frith. The first two stages, the magical and the logographic (picture) stage, are illustrated by writing. For example, the child does not know the relationship between letters and their sounds and, when asked to write a word, just engages in scribbling and passes it off as writing. The other example Frith gives in the model relating to writing is a logographic one. The child can write *dog* but cannot analyze the phonology of the letters or the letter sequence. If the same word is typed in a different font than the child's handwriting, the child refuses to recognize that this is the same word. The typed word *dog* does not contain the same features as the child's handwritten *dog*. Not only is the word being read as a picture, but the details of the "handwritten" picture assume importance.

Think of a child who does not know how to write but is asked to say the spelling of a word (*hat* or *mat* or *dog*). Can he/she follow a logographic image? We think not. Saying the spelling of a word requires the child to say the letters one by one in the right sequence, as opposed to seeing a whole picture. So is it possible that children cannot have a logographic stage in spelling? Do we have a whole word spelling and a spelling based on phonological analysis of the word, just as in reading? It is possible that the child remembers the word *dog* as a whole or as a gestalt pattern and then draws it, letter by letter, just as a picture is drawn? On the other hand, if the child is forced to write out the word letter by letter, he/she must say the name of the letters; then it becomes the same kind of activity as phonological coding.

In one sense though, children could be learning to spell whole words without doing phonological analysis. They cannot perform orthographic or morphological (word) groupings such as *save* or *saved*. Let us examine the orthographic features of the word *bead* compared to the word *dead*; children must remember that the two are orthographically similar in the middle part but are pronounced differently. If children cannot distinguish the different pronunciations of words which share common orthography, they really do not understand spelling. The challenge, especially in the English language, is to learn logographic features.

Are There Rules to Spelling?

So, how does a child learn to spell by phonological analysis? Do children use the same strategies as they would when asked to spell new words (for example, *reticent*) or even pseudo-words (for example, *oldier*)? There are many ways in which we can answer this question.

First, let us look at the different ways children approach spelling. Children who have already had some instruction in reading, writing, and spelling, and are deemed good spellers, will spell very familiar words automatically. The spelling is known so well that when they see a card on which the word is written with one of the letters misplaced, their reaction typically is, "It doesn't look right!" This kind of strategy could be called automatic, that is, the children are spelling the words without much effort. The words are well rehearsed in terms of their spelling. Such children, as well as adults, sometimes use a technique to check the spelling of a certain word by writing it and deciding whether or not it looks right.

A second strategy used in spelling is *phonological* analysis, that is, breaking the word down into segments and then writing each segment. Once children have learned to do this, they can change a word they have spelled to a new word, whose spelling they may not know, by adding prefixes or suffixes. For example, having learned to spell the word *typical*, they can spell *atypical* just by adding a prefix, or *typicality* by adding the suffix *ity*. Adding bits and pieces to a word and thus changing it is called *morphology*. We learn to spell many words by making morphological changes, such as adding *ed* to many verbs to change them into the past tense. For example, *braid–braided, allude–alluded*. However, children have to remember when not to add *ed* to convert the word to its past tense. Examples of irregular past tenses abound: *slept, went, stole*, and *met* rather than *sleeped*, and so on. Specific transformations of a word can change its meaning by the form of its past tense. For example, the noun *ground* can be used as a verb with *grounded* as its past tense but *ground* is also the past tense of the verb *to grind*.

The examples given illustrate two of the strategies for learning to spell. The addition of *ed* for a past tense is the *applying a rule* strategy. Examples of other rules used for changing the spelling of a word are the addition of *ing* (*come–coming*), not doubling the consonant immediately before the vowel if the word ends in one, and so on. This is why the teacher in elementary school sometimes drills rules into the head of the young speller. But sometimes the young spellers themselves can figure out the rules and say them back to the teacher unsolicited.

The example given of the word *ground*, which can be a noun or a verb or the past tense of the verb *to grind*, requires comprehension, or *semantic knowledge*. We may wonder whether the semantic characteristics of the word are at all important for spelling since a great number of words can be spelled even if children do not know their meanings. There are many instances where the meaning of the word assists in spelling it. Take the word *man*; we can spell *manly*, *manned*, *human*, and *humane*. If we know the meaning of these words it becomes easier to remember the spelling. How do I spell *lassitude*? Does it have anything to do with the word *lass*, which is a girl? Is the word *aptitude* derived from *apt*? We know that *humidity* has a root which has the component *h-u-m* but the same component is present in *humour* or *exhume*. The semantic strategies that are helpful with spelling probably appear at a later stage than automatic, phonological, morphological, or even rule-governed strategies.

Does the word *rational* have anything to do with the word *ratio*? If we know that it does, all we have to remember is to write ratio and add *nal*. (Did the Greeks really mean that a rational person knows ratios? Was that person logical and mathematical?)

To recapitulate—a word has to be sounded out, but for fluent writing or spelling it must be written automatically and without effort. We learn spelling by using consistent rules. Contrary to widespread belief, a great deal of English spelling is quite consistent, although there are a number of irregular words. Thus, spelling is rule-governed, but irregular words such as *know* and *tongue* have to be remembered as *logographs* or pictures. The logographic strategy is not, then, left behind as an anachronism when we learn to spell phonologically or by applying spelling rules. We also use meaning, semantic knowledge in other words, to help us spell. These strategies help us enormously to spell words which we have never seen in writing or which are used infrequently.

How does a Child with Dyslexia Cope with Spelling?

If the major disadvantage of dyslexia is its effect on a child's ability to do phonological analysis, does the dyslexic child use the methods discussed for spelling? It is true that the child with dyslexia, or young readers who do not know the spelling of a word, cannot translate the whole word into its orthographic units while writing it. For example, having seen the word *beach* frequently written at a seaside resort, a child with dyslexia, like any other child, may learn to write it as a whole word. A child with dyslexia can also be helped by a semantic analysis of the word. If a child understands the sentence *A large whale beached in Santa Monica last night*, he/she is more likely to spell the word *beached*.

The dyslexic child may recognize a word but may not be able to produce it in writing. Thus, any remedial program that aims at correcting dyslexia should incorporate both reading and spelling remedial methods. Spelling can be oral or written. The relation between spelling and writing, and the nature of writing itself are the next issues that we discuss.

Spelling and Writing

Writing uses words and letters which are the basic ingredients of spelling. However, the majority of dyslexics are poor readers and may have problems in both reading and writing. The process of writing involves at least two main activities that combine to make it possible. One is the physical act of forming letters and words. Handwriting used to be an important component of writing but with the use of typewriters and now word processors the role of handwriting in writing or spelling has decreased. Nevertheless, schoolchildren all over the world still start their formal education with handwriting. The second activity is the creation of a text which will be discussed later.

The mechanics of handwriting can be daunting for very young children. The teacher complains that the child is messy and does not write neatly. The mother may complain that the child is too young to even hold the pen or pencil properly and to put it on paper. In many developing, upwardly-mobile societies, children as young as three-and-a-half years of age are taught to write, which may well start them on the path of messy writing. Surprisingly, however, some children have such control over their hands that they are able to write neatly even at this age. These children may become models to other children for whom the act of writing presents an enormous barrier to acquiring literacy. Literacy is not about the ability to write the letters of the alphabet, yet, both literally and figuratively, writing assumes major importance in the early acquisition of literacy. One begins to wonder where the emphasis lies in teaching a child to acquire elements of literacy.

Writing: A Physical Activity and the Construction of Text

One of the two major components of writing is the physical aspect of forming written words and letters. This can be compared to the physical aspect of speaking. Just as a fluent speaker must be able to articulate fast enough and clearly enough to be understood, so must a fluent writer be able to write legibly and with reasonably good speed. In the previous section we discussed how spelling could be done orally as well as by writing down the letters and words. Oral spelling is not enough. Children have to leave a permanent record on paper, of their ability to communicate, so that these records can be examined and corrected. All of this contributes to the acquisition of language skills. Thus, one of the major difficulties of a dyslexic child may be clumsiness in writing. While spelling is dependent on cognitive processes such as sequencing or successive processing, writing, in addition to these, requires *planning*. Children have to put together a motor program for producing written impressions on paper. In the case of handwriting, the motor program is distinctly different from the thoughts or ideas that are ultimately expressed in writing. Therefore, the second important aspect of writing is the *creation of a text*. Creating a text that is found in a sentence or a paragraph, and later in essays, requires the knowledge of grammar as well as strategies for putting down one's thoughts and ideas.

Writing Composition and Oral Narration Need Planning

But are these not the requirements of oral speech as well? When children are asked to describe an event, to retell a story or tell an original one, they have to generate thoughts and ideas in a coherent manner. In any kind of meaningful oral narration, the role of planning assumes great importance. Without it the oral narrative loses its focus and, ultimately, even its meaning. We have heard of disorganized speech even in healthy adults and there are many children who are struggling with not only the gathering of ideas for communication but also in getting together the means of written production. The two aspects of writing are expressed in the technical terms translation or *transcription* and *text generation*. Transcription by itself is like a spelling skill. We discussed earlier how both children and adults may know the spelling of a long word but still make mistakes when putting it down on paper. This is mainly due to the length of the word. The working memory is stressed when the word is too long to remember, resulting in children omitting some of the letters, especially in the middle of the word.

Many Cognitive Processes Compete with Each Other in Writing

The physical act of forming the letters in handwritten spellings further challenges the child's abilities and resources, and adds to the stress on the working memory. Translation or transcription, then, has both a cognitive load and a demand on motor ability. Children may put so much effort into the sheer act of transcription that the quality of their writing becomes poor. They write only brief sentences or paragraphs when asked to produce a written text. The ideas in the paragraph may not be presented coherently as the energy available to the child is taken up by the act of writing itself. This is perhaps the main reason why dyslexic children can speak coherently and fluently, expressing their ideas well, but when asked to write, fail the test miserably. As children grow older they learn the three Rs (Reading, Writing, and Arithmetic) in school and most of them acquire the basic mechanics of writing by the age of 10. The higher mental processes of *planning* (using the strategies of *focusing* on some ideas and not on others) and *revising* what one has written may then become apparent in their writing. However, children with dyslexia often have poor spelling and writing skills and may not master the techniques of writing by the age of ten. Therefore, it is unfair to judge their ability for communication from their written efforts. We have to remember while teaching children who experience dyslexia, especially those who are poor in reading and spelling, that although spelling is a necessary component of literacy, emphasis on the mechanics of handwriting should be reduced.

To which part of the brain does writing belong? We will end this chapter with an answer to this question.

What can Neuropsychology Tell Us about Spelling and Writing?

The relationship between spelling and writing needs to be clarified, and a good place to begin is with the distinction between spelling and writing in neuropsychology. Why neuropsychology? Neuropsychological bases relate to the functional differences between spelling and writing in different regions of the brain. Therefore, the connection between spelling and writing in the context of neuropsychology becomes quite important. There is no doubt that spelling and writing are different because the functional organizations of spelling and writing are not only separate but also located in different parts of the brain. To understand the distinction between spelling and writing, let us first begin by thinking of spelling as related to the reading process.

There are at least two different opinions regarding the relationship between spelling and speech. One suggests that there is a separate brain area for motor skills related to writing. This is true. The selective impairment of spelling skills without any impairment of writing skills is now well established. The second opinion is that the disorder of spelling is similar to that of reading. Children can read by sound, which is phonological coding, or by sight, which is reading a word as a whole without sounding it out. In spelling there are three different ways of conceptualizing the main processes, two of which correspond to the processes used for reading. *Spelling by sound* corresponds to phonological coding and *vocabulary-based spelling* corresponds to sight reading or "direct visual access". These two have been distinguished in neurologically impaired patients

as well. Some patients show an inability for spelling-by-sound even
as their ability for vocabulary-based spelling is intact, while in others
the abilities are reversed. However, there is a third kind of spelling disorder called *spelling assembly*, which is the inability to put
letters in the right sequence while spelling. Even though the person may be able to spell phonologically and by direct visual access,
the sequencing of letters can be especially impaired. The patients
make errors in the order of letters and with letter substitution,
and these mostly occur in the middle part of the word. This is to
be expected as sequencing or successive processing is involved in
serial learning. Words in the middle part of the list are the least remembered as compared to those at the beginning or at the end.

Thus, there are three ways of looking at spelling if we consider
spelling and writing together. The three different aspects of spelling just described would be reflected differently in writing. As
mentioned earlier, we could conceptualize the whole process of
spelling as similar to the process of word recognition. Let us go
through it step by step: a target word could be spelled from vocabulary or from sound. Whatever method is used, the spelling has
to be assembled, and therein might be a difficulty in writing the
letters sequentially. But writing is only one of the output modes.
Assembling is, in itself, a cognitive function leading to *written
output*, *oral output*, or a computer or typing output (for a detailed
discussion, see McCarthy and Warrington, 1990).

The Movements in Writing

The motor activity of writing is a specific kind of voluntary movement. Children or adults who have difficulty in fine and gross
motor coordination would also have difficulty in writing. However,
this does not always happen. A person may not be able to imitate
certain kinds of movements, gestures, and so on, but, nevertheless,
their writing ability could be intact. The execution part in writing,
as discussed before, is transcription. Therefore, it depends on an
intact motor pattern for producing letters. If writing is a reflection
of the motor activity, then we could see difficulties in at least two
distinct procedures. One is the "letter form" selection, that is, the

organization of movements that are necessary to write the letters of the alphabet and connect them in a word. Children who have this kind of difficulty may not be able to take dictation at all, or may have problems in simply converting a word or a sentence written in block capitals to handwriting. Crowding and spacing are the other problems. Writing is crowded on one side of the page leaving an excessively wide margin, or extra strokes are added while writing such letters as *m*, *n*, and *u*. Spacing errors are best described as leaving big gaps between the letters of a word.

In terms of brain anatomy, writing disorders are very difficult to localize because they could be caused by many different factors as we discussed. Neuropsychologists believe that writing is a specific form of motor activity that can be separated from a general deterioration of voluntary movements found in some people (McCarthy and Warrington, 1990). Many believe that the act of writing may be drawing upon a specific set of motor patterns that are stored in the brain.

II

Remediation of Reading and Learning Difficulties

7

Theory and Practice

Remediation is not instruction. We begin by thinking about remediation and how it differs from instruction. Instruction is what happens in the school in a classroom. The teachers instruct or formally teach children. Although there are many ways to teach children, the essence of teaching is transferring knowledge. The teacher has the knowledge and the problem in instruction is how to transfer this knowledge to the child. This is not a very simple affair.

Instruction has at least four different components. The teacher instructs a *learner* so the characteristics of the learner determine to some extent both the manner of instruction as well as the successful outcome. Then there is the *teacher*. He or she also has certain modes and manners that affect the outcome of instruction. The learner and the teacher are in a particular *setting*—this is the school. The school may be of good or poor quality. It may be in a slum area or in a wealthy suburb. Accordingly, the school may or may not have adequate resources (tape recorders, slide projectors, computers, and so on) to engage the children in various activities. Finally, there is the *curriculum* and its content. So effective instruction depends on all these four components. Many teachers know that if the object of instruction is merely to put some kind of information into the heads of the pupils, like pouring water into an empty jug, teaching will not be very successful. The characteristics of the learner must be considered. For example, a 7-year-old child is asked by a friendly teacher, "Why is it so hard for you to pay attention to the lessons after recess?" He replies, "You see, I try to choose a friend to play with during recess. I try hard and look for the right boy but by the time I make up my mind, the recess is over. That leaves me tired and thinking."

Sometimes children do not understand the purpose of instruction. A teacher is trying to teach the basic concepts of addition and subtraction to a 7-year-old: "You see, John, suppose you have five pieces of candy. Your best friend gives you two more pieces. You now have seven. But then you give away six pieces of candy to your little sister. Then you have one." The child says, "But ... but ... Miss Kelly, that is called sharing!"

Remediation is not instruction. Only when instruction has failed does remediation take over. Instruction is typically given to a large number of children in a classroom. The instructor in the classroom cannot take into account only an individual child's learning style, maturation, and case history. Instruction does not aim at removing the deficit or difficulty the child may be experiencing for some very specific reasons. It treats children as a community of learners in a classroom. The purpose of remediation is, of course, to help the child compensate for difficulties that he/she has. As the word suggests, it is aimed at correcting the problem. For best results, remediation has to be individualized. Of course, we know that in some schools where special and regular children share the same classroom, individualized programming of special children is adopted. In those circumstances, instruction and remediation are merged, but, generally speaking, remediation is aimed at ameliorating the difficulties, reducing the deficits, and correcting maladaptive strategies that a learner may have. Remediation, therefore, goes beyond the surface difficulties. If a child does not know how to swim, the remedy is not to throw him into the water and let him sink or swim. Similarly, if a child is poor in spelling, remediation would not recommend more and more spelling exercises.

The Roots of Remediation

Consider PREP (PASS Reading Enhancement Program), its roots and assumptions. First of all, PREP assumes that children's difficulties in learning can be modified, reduced, and improved through appropriate cognitive stimulation, that is, the child has an enormous potential for learning, only some of which is exploited in regular classroom instruction. It also assumes that if the child is appropriately treated from the beginning, these unused potentials can be developed and the possibility of a learning deficit can be avoided.

The inspiration for modifying the child's cognitive functions comes from studies on early stimulation, first done on animals and later on young children. It was shown by Donald Hebb and his colleagues in Canada (Das, 1973) that even rats can improve in learning to get around mazes and solving problems if they are reared in an environment that provides a number of recreational activities, such as swings and slides, and problems to be solved in an indoor living setting. In contrast, rats that are brought up in a deprived environment, within the four walls of a little cage, do not seem to be able to learn quickly. This led to the idea of early stimulation of potentially disadvantaged children. In spite of the many controversies surrounding its effectiveness, the belief that human beings are plastic and that intelligence is malleable encouraged the early Headstart programs. (Headstart is a program of the United States Department of Health and Human Services, that provides comprehensive education, health, nutrition, and parent involvement services to low-income children and their families.) Let us understand one thing clearly: providing a culturally rich environment for children who are otherwise disadvantaged by poverty and unfavorable family circumstances is the right thing to do. It does not matter if early education programs do not result in improvement of intelligence on standardized IQ tests (Das, 1973; Haywood and Tapp, 1966).

Another line of thinking that has influenced the construction of remedial programs is based on how we have been able to train individuals with mental retardation to increase their memory. One form of training involved teaching strategies to remember a series of numbers or simple words. The strategies included listening carefully to each number or word as it was spoken, mentally rehearsing the words or numbers, and then trying to recall the series. This strategy training was quite successful in increasing the span of memory for individuals with mental retardation. However, there was a problem. Those who were trained to use this strategy could not easily and automatically transfer what they had learned from their previous experience to a new task. It would be unrealistic to train them every time they were given a new task. Nevertheless, the experience did show that even moderately mentally handicapped individuals can learn to use strategies for a specific task.

Strategy training was not perhaps the best way to teach these individuals to increase their mental capacity or sharpen their cognitive functions. Direct teaching of strategies requires the learner to both remember and apply the rules when faced with a new situation, and also to determine whether the situation calls for the application of the rules. For example, if the words are related to each other, it may not be necessary to remember them one by one. Rather, remembering the cluster of words that are related would be a more economic strategy. This is what the individuals with mental retardation needed to understand but could not. Such flexibility in using a strategy may come easily to children with normal intelligence and to most learning-disabled children, but not to those with mental retardation.

Therefore, a different way of learning has to be encouraged, one that is inductive, as opposed to the learning described earlier which is deductive. In the new kind of learning that we are proposing, the child goes through a specific task that requires the use of certain strategies but is never directly told what the strategies are. The child discovers them, guided by the structure of the task. As the child performs more of these tasks, strategies develop almost unconsciously, that is, the child begins to understand the principles that must be used to solve the task. For example, in a task that involves sequencing (remembering a series of digits or words in sequence), the child must learn to rehearse, but when the list is too long for memorizing at one stretch, the child must learn how to "chunk" or cluster the words. For instance, if the words are *cat*, *man*, *tea*, *wall*, *hot*, *shoe*, and *girl*, the child may learn to chunk them into groups of three, thereby remembering the whole series easily. In this way, children develop their own ways of dealing with such a task. In this inductive type of learning, rules are not given by the teacher, who does not know which way would be the best for a particular child, but discovered and used, sometimes unconsciously, by the learner.

Mediation and Internalization in PREP

Allowing the child to discover the rules with the help of a teacher or an instructor is a standard procedure in our program. If the child cannot work out those rules by him or herself, they are internalized by the child through the mediation of the instructor. The teacher, then, becomes a facilitator. Instruction becomes a combination of the teacher's interaction with the learner and the learner's discovery of the tricks for doing the task. Vygotsky (1978) was a great advocate of guided discovery learning, where the child is helped through prompting, but only in accordance with his needs. Eventually, through the mediation of the adult, the principles of the tasks, such as sequencing or successive processing, become internalized. So, internalization and mediation become the two central activities that help children to learn, and the two modes of thinking that the teacher tries to facilitate.

Ideally, therefore, children in a good remedial program are engaged as *active learners* and as *reflective learners*. They are engaged in the activity and think about what they are doing. This has been the common procedure intended in many remediation programs, but the theory behind it has not always been clear. This lack of understanding may result in a mechanical approach being promoted.

The interaction between the child and the teacher is framed within social cognition, that is, remediation becomes a collaborative activity. The instructor and the child work together, attempting to understand each other's intentions and modifying their activities accordingly. All learning, as Vygotsky said, is a sociocultural act. (And hence, ZPD [Zone of Proximal Development] is often quoted as the central point of remediation following Vygotsky.) We transmit culture through such collaborative activities, and rightly so, because human civilization is based on the transmission of cultural knowledge acquired in one's own generation to the next generation. A remedial procedure, therefore, reflects the world of cultural transmission in a microcosm.

Conclusion

What we have discussed is a long-winded answer to the question, "Is there a remedy for learning disabilities?" To summarize—the answer is yes, there is a remedy, but, first of all, the cognitive processes that may be lacking for learning to read must be recognized. Tasks and situations that promote the use of the cognitive strategies must be designed carefully so that they provide a structure for the discovery of strategies to occur. The strategies may vary from individual to individual and, therefore, there is no one correct strategy that needs to be taught. This is a departure from the usual teaching mode where there is only one right answer. The teacher's role is to facilitate the discovery of whatever strategy works for the child. The child is actively engaged in this search and also reflects on the activity with the collaboration of the teacher.

I end this chapter by presenting a theoretical introduction for PREP.

Know the Ropes

We are sailing deep into the theoretical sea of PREP. Without knowing the ropes, our sailing will be endless and the journey indeterminate. It is, therefore, essential to discuss the four roots, the three philosophies, two examples, and the overarching spirit of PREP (see Figure 7.1).

Figure 7.1   Know the Ropes of PREP

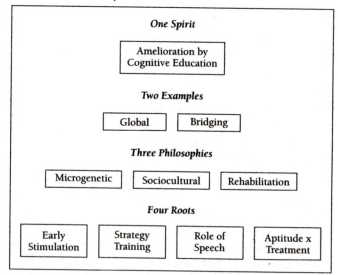

Source: Author. Based on the ideas of Hebb, Vygotsky, and Luria.

Let us consolidate the sources of inspiration, the roots that sustain PREP, as discussed in the previous section (see Figure 7.1). Three of the roots—early stimulation, strategy training, and ZPD have been described earlier. What has not been described is the *aptitude x treatment* interaction. Teachers and academic therapists instinctively feel that they should take advantage of the child's special aptitudes and design their instructional program accordingly. In the case of PREP, we recommend that the child's strengths and weaknesses in cognitive processes be determined first. Then, by exposing the child to a set of tasks that can be attempted either simultaneously or successively, he/she is left free to use whatever strategies are most comfortable. The tasks are designed in such a way that the child is encouraged to try out strategies, see how they work, and be flexible enough to change the strategies for a successful resolution of the task. Children do not have to be aware of exactly what strategy they are using at any given moment; they can instead covertly change from one strategy to another as they are exposed to the various tasks in the program.

The three philosophies guide us to a better understanding of the roots of PREP. The first philosophy is *microgenetic*, that is, observing in small ways how change in behavior occurs as the child is going through a learning experience. We should not forget that for the child remediation is, after all, a learning experience and it is important to know not only when changes in behavior may take place, but how the changes happen.

The same child changes his or her behavior while performing a task from time to time, even within the same training session. The child's strategies shift and blend. The conditions that produce change in strategies reside in the child at least as much as in the task itself.

Children have many strategies available to them while doing a task and these strategies are in competition with each other. The competition can be resolved with practice as the child learns to attempt the task in the way most suited to his or her background and temperament. "Micro" means small and "genetic" is the birth or the beginning of a change. So rather than looking at the big changes noticed at the end of the solution to a task, we recommend following some authorities in this area, who recommend that small changes in the child's activities be observed and recorded to learn more about his/her approach to the task.

Strategies are plans and, therefore, observation regarding change, in small ways, allows us to look through a window into the planning process of the child. "In small proportions we just beauties see; And in short measures, life may perfect be." For our purposes we may replace *beauties* with *changes*, and *life* with *learning*.

The second philosophy that will help us understand PREP originates with Vygotsky, who made two very thoughtful suggestions. One has to do with disability of any kind, not only reading disability. Disability is not a defect; it is rather an opportunity to be creative. The idea that a child with a learning disability or cognitive deficit only compensates for that deficit reinforces the tendency of the teacher to believe that the child has to be like a so-called normal child in all respects. Thus, according to Vygotsky, disability should not be regarded as a negative label. The disabled person already has a handicap; society and culture need not increase the burden by looking at the individual as being in some way inferior to the so-called normal person. The second important opinion of Vygotsky concerns learning itself. Learning always occurs in a sociocultural setting and having originated from that setting, the learned behavior influences that sociocultural environment. Thus a dialectical relationship exists between the two. Individuals with reading difficulties may come from a nonliterate culture, an environment in which books, magazines, and reading are not positively encouraged. Rather than encouraging such individuals to feel that they lack something, which contributes to low self-esteem, the PREP program gently orients them to the culture of literacy (Vygotsky, 1978). The final philosophical orientation of PREP is focused on reorganization and substitution. A particular cognitive process may be defective, or the child may be lacking the ability to process information in a sequence. This does not mean that we should, in frustration, give up on the child. The message from Luria (1973) and others who have worked on neurologically impaired patients' rehabilitation is that opportunities for substituting the defective process and replacing it with a process that is intact, such as simultaneous processing and planning, should provide the appropriate philosophical orientation for remediation. The emphasis is not on what is absent, but on what is intact (see Figure 7.2).

Figure 7.2   The Three Philosophies of PREP

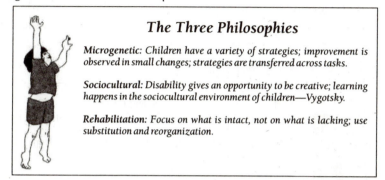

The Three Philosophies

Microgenetic: Children have a variety of strategies; improvement is observed in small changes; strategies are transferred across tasks.

Sociocultural: Disability gives an opportunity to be creative; learning happens in the sociocultural environment of children—Vygotsky.

Rehabilitation: Focus on what is intact, not on what is lacking; use substitution and reorganization.

Source: Author.

So where does that leave us in regard to the old question—should we teach to strengthen, or to remove the weakness? The answer, as always, is both. Teaching to strengthen takes advantage of our knowledge of the deficient functions in the child and thus helps the child to substitute, replace, and reorganize. In this way the child is motivated to learn new strategies. If successive processing is weak, the child takes advantage of his/her strengths in the other processes, such as planning and simultaneous processing. Indeed, minute observation of children who are poor in successive processing shows that when they are engaged in PREP tasks that ordinarily require successive processing, they can sometimes cope with them quite adequately. Such children are sometimes able to get around the difficulty in sequencing by chunking the chain of objects or letters into groups of two or three, similar to bite-size units, which they can then handle simultaneously.

Each task in the PREP program has a global and a bridging component, that is, two examples. The global component shows the way to be followed in reading and spelling-related learning. The global task lays down the purpose of the training task, and creates the right conditions for the child to be curious and to be surprised. Psychologists say that the global task enables the child to understand what is required by letting him or her transfer the whole action to a mental representation.

Encouraging the child to talk his or her way through, doing the task and paying attention to his or her self-talk, can provide insights into how the child is transforming the activity to a mental representation (see Figure 7.3).

Figure 7.3   Three Teaching Approaches

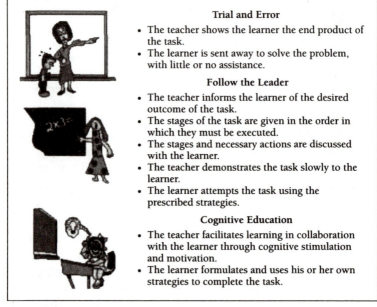

Trial and Error

- The teacher shows the learner the end product of the task.
- The learner is sent away to solve the problem, with little or no assistance.

Follow the Leader

- The teacher informs the learner of the desired outcome of the task.
- The stages of the task are given in the order in which they must be executed.
- The stages and necessary actions are discussed with the learner.
- The teacher demonstrates the task slowly to the learner.
- The learner attempts the task using the prescribed strategies.

Cognitive Education

- The teacher facilitates learning in collaboration with the learner through cognitive stimulation and motivation.
- The learner formulates and uses his or her own strategies to complete the task.

Source: Author.

First the child might say aloud, "Oh, I need to do this, not that, because that didn't work last time. What the heck! Let me try. If it doesn't work, I'll try a different way." This external speech is later replaced by internal speech, where the child is secretly, as it were, speaking to himself or herself. The global tasks are interesting and easy, make the child confident, and ensure success in the bridging tasks that follow. There are no external rewards and punishments. When the child fails to accomplish the task in a certain way, there is an opportunity to search for a new solution. The motivation here is internal, that is, it comes from within the child. PREP has only one uniting spirit (Gal'perin, 1982).

By using PREP with children or adults, we are trying to improve their cognitive functioning. The entire approach of PREP can be broadly described as cognitive education or educating the individual in the business of knowing. Sometimes this goes a step further, to educating the individual in learning how to know and how to acquire knowledge.

Now that we know the ropes, the rest falls into its place and the sailing is smooth.

Note: Further readings for those interested—Gal'perin (1982), Kuhn (1995), Luria (1963), Siegler and Crowley (1991), and Stein (1988).

8

COGENT Program: Getting
Ready to Read

"Reading is the process of understanding speech written down. The goal is to gain access to meaning." (Ziegler and Goswami, 2005: 3)

Good readers not only understand how print is a representation of speech, but also use knowledge (language, life experiences, and so on) to derive meaning from what they read. While speaking develops naturally when children live in a culture and a community that uses language and where children are expected to interact with others, reading must be taught. Thus, if instruction is appropriate for the acquisition of reading, we could expect children who do not exhibit genetic or neurodevelopmental impairments to be reading after three years of schooling. Yet, a substantial proportion of children are not reading after such a period of formal instruction. Nonacademic factors, such as a genetic deficit, certain types of neurological impairments, or chronic malnutrition that adversely affects brain development, are more difficult to prevent and rectify than faults in instruction, or the lack of adequate facilities and procedures for the early diagnosis and intervention of reading difficulties. The COGENT (Cognitive Enhancement Training) program aims at building the cognitive, language, and phonemic awareness skills that support reading, especially for those children who are at risk for developing reading difficulties.

In the present chapter, we describe the Reading Readiness program called COGENT (Das, 2004). But before we do that, let us step back and look at the entire landscape of how children learn to read. The simple answer is—by learning the letters of the alphabet, learning that a letter has a sound, combining the sounds of the letters in simple words, and all the other things that children are taught by their teachers in Grade 1. However, does this work all the time for all students? Letter to sound is not a simple conversion; as we all know, the letter *a* may be said in many different ways (for example, *apple*, *air*, *autumn*). Sometimes when children are learning letter–sound correspondence, they cannot break down the word into its sounds. They need to perceive the sounds in the first place, that is, they have to pay attention and discriminate between the different sounds, and then organize the sounds in a sequence. They must also blend the sounds together, chunk the sounds into bite-size units, and assemble the chunks in units that can be pronounced. Then they have to vocalize or say the word. Children are paying attention, planning and organizing an output, chunking, and sequencing. Planning, attention, and the two ways of ordering information into simultaneous and successive types (PASS) are the four basic processes that we need not only for reading, but for getting around in a town, understanding a conversation, thinking of the future, or, in short, living our lives. The challenge for educators is to prepare the children for reading by allowing them to apply these processes, to make them ready to attend to words and language, discriminate between sounds in a word, automatically recognize not only familiar shapes and colors but also letters and simple words, follow the sequence of arrangement of words in a sentence, and, what is more, understand, comprehend, and realize how the words are arranged in a sentence, sentences in a text, and texts within a theme. As children get ready to do all this, they are ready to read and are on the path to enjoying reading.

COGENT is an attempt to create a program for reading readiness by first ensuring that children are engaged in PASS processes, a prerequisite for reading. It is based on knowledge borrowed from several reliable studies (Luria, 1981). It is based on evidence, and now we are also building research evidence for its efficacy and to show that it works.

Development of the COGENT Program

COGENT is based on the PASS theory of intelligence (Das, Naglieri and Kirby, 1994). As discussed earlier in this book, the PASS theory proposes that cognition is organized into three systems. The planning system is responsible for controlling and organizing behavior. The attention system is responsible for alertness, maintaining arousal levels, and assuring focus on appropriate stimuli. The processing system employs simultaneous and successive processes to encode, transform, and retain information. In simultaneous processing, information is coded so that relations among items can be seen and information integrated. In successive processing, information is coded so that the only links between items are sequential in nature.

PASS Constructs—A Summary for Teachers

Attention prepares us to select and to focus on what is relevant. An attentive child does not get distracted easily and at the same time shifts attention when it is necessary. Children differ in their strength of attention.

Planning is deciding on a course of action to achieve a goal. It is the first stage for problem solving. It involves strategies for a solution and thinking before acting. When doing a task, a good planner evaluates the course of his or her action, anticipates problems, and takes appropriate steps to correct the course of action.

There are two coding processes—*Simultaneous* and *Successive*. We get a medley of information, which needs synthesis to enable the processing of information simultaneously. A common pattern must be seen when we group the different bits of information that we wish to analyze and see the relationship between them simultaneously. Some children are good at finding such a common connection among designs and figures, and even among ideas expressed in a sentence. They see the whole without getting lost in the parts. Some other children cannot do this very well.

At other times, we are frequently called upon to arrange information in a sequence. At no time though can we see the entire chain of events, words, or ideas. This ability to arrange information successively is essential in memorizing a list of unrelated words and for speaking fluently. Children differ in their capacity for following a sequence of actions or remembering what came after what. After witnessing a series of events or the words in a sentence or passage, some children are good at repeating it in sequence. They are good at successive processing.

When you read the description of the five modules of COGENT later, watch how far each of the following operations is present in the tasks that the children are asked to do. In each module, children are engaged in three main mental activities—they perceive, they remember, and they must think and conceptualize (Das, Kirby and Jarman, 1975). Let us elaborate these operations in one of the modules.

In Module 1, children are asked to squeeze a ball once whenever the teacher shows a picture of a small animal, squeeze twice when the picture shows a big animal, but not squeeze at all when a flower is shown. The animal pictures include a whale, an elephant, a butterfly, and a cat.

- *Perceive*: Children have to look at the picture with all its features.
- *Remember*: As soon as they have looked at it, they reach into their memory, recall images of the animal if they have seen one before or other pictures of the same animal even though none of them look exactly the same, then recognize it, and give it a name. Upon recognizing it, they are also reminded of many things about that animal, but they must focus on its size—is it a big animal or a small one?
- *Think and Conceptualize*: What am I supposed to do? How am I going to respond? Oh, yes, squeeze the ball once because it is a butterfly. It is really a little animal, although in the picture, it looks the same size as the elephant. Oh well, this is tricky because all the pictures are the same size!

The four cognitive processes are used in each one of those mental operations. First things first—children have to pay attention to what the teacher is showing them. *Attention!* The picture has to be recognized and placed in the class of either big or small animals. *Simultaneous processing!* Then, children have to plan how many times they need to squeeze the ball; squeeze the ball according to their inner voice—Hey! This is a big animal, squeeze, squeeze. *Planning!*

The teacher goes on changing the pictures faster and faster. Children have to maintain their rhythm of squeezes, squeeze faster and faster, in sequence, as the pictures are shown. *Successive processing*!

Some children may be good at one kind of processing but not so good at another. But all mental activities use each of these processes to some extent; some need more, some less. Cognitive enhancement is a term for promoting the processes, making it easier for children to do the mental operations that are appropriate, to make a habit of using the processes quickly without much effort. COGENT helps the children to use the processes in academic work.

COGENT should benefit cognitive growth, typically of developing children as well as children with special needs, such as those with limited exposure to literacy, mild developmental delay, language impairment, and those at risk for developing dyslexia and other learning difficulties. The program is suitable for classroom instruction as well as for one-on-one and small group training in clinical and educational settings.

9

A Taste of COGENT: Program Modules

Module 1: Squeeze and Say

The overall objective is to help students attend to instructions from an outside agent (that is, a teacher or facilitator) and then internalize those instructions. The student's task is to follow an increasingly complex set of rules given by the facilitator. Initially, students are only required to provide a motor response (for example, when you see a picture of an animal, squeeze your hand twice; when you see a picture of a flower, squeeze your hand once). The second level of difficulty requires both a motor and verbal response with time constraints (for example, when you see a picture of an animal, squeeze your hand twice and say "squeeze-squeeze"; when you see a picture of a flower, squeeze your hand once and say "squeeze"). The highest level of difficulty requires students to respond to and differentiate an increasing number of stimuli without picture support (for example, when I say an animal name that is long you say squeeze-squeeze and squeeze twice, and when I say an animal name that is short you say squeeze and squeeze your hand once). This process is then applied to distinguish the syllable length of nonsense words (for example, when I say a silly word that is long, you say "long-squeeze-squeeze" and squeeze twice; when I say a silly word that is short, you say "short-squeeze" and squeeze once). Students are given opportunities to create their own exemplars in many of the activities and share these with their classmates.

Module 2: Clap and Listen

Aspects of phonological awareness and working memory (phonological discrimination, phonological memory, rhyming, and analysis of sounds in words and syllables) are the focus of Module 2. The student's task is to respond to and discriminate smaller units of speech (that is, words and syllables) presented in progressively longer and faster sequences. For example, students listen to a series of words/syllables and when they hear a word/syllable that is different from the rest in the sequence, they clap their hands. At first the words/syllables are phonemically dissimilar (for example, *sun, sun, **book**, sun; ba, ba, ba, **jee***), and then they become phonemically similar (for example, *gate, gate, **kate**, gate; ta, ta, **ka**, ta*). At the next level of difficulty, the frequency of presentation is increased. At the highest level of difficulty, students produce the words/syllables sequences themselves. As in Module 1, students are given opportunities to create their own exemplars in many of the activities and share these with their classmates.

Module 3: Funny Relatives

In Module 3, the student's task is to indicate first the syntagmatic and then the paradigmatic relationships described by the facilitator. At the easiest level of difficulty, students place two objects in relation to each other in response to syntagmatic sentence constructions provided by the facilitator. The students demonstrate both the action and the spatial relationship expressed in each sentence (For example, *The kitten jumped onto the table. The kitten is hiding under the table.*). The students also respond to questions asked by the facilitator, which include both syntagmatic and paradigmatic relationships (For example, "Tell me what the kitten is doing. Why do you think the kitten is hiding?"). The level of difficulty is increased through expanding the length and complexity of facilitator utterances and phasing out the picture cues (For example, Sally and John want to have breakfast. Sally said, "We must have eggs for breakfast." John said, "We don't have any eggs, we must go to the store." What do Sally and John want for breakfast? Where do they have to go to get the eggs?).

Module 4: Name Game

Module 4 focuses on onset and rhyme analysis. The student's task is to discriminate onsets and rhymes. At the easiest level, students articulate onsets or rhymes depending on the facilitator instructions (For example, "I'm going to tell you about a very cute little baby I met. You know when babies are learning how to talk they can only say the first sound of words. When the little baby wanted a drink of water she said w-w-w. I want to see if you can tell me how the baby would say some other words. If the baby wanted some cake what would she say? If the baby saw a fish how would she say fish?"). At the next level of difficulty, students use puppets to articulate both onsets and rhymes. One of the puppets always eats onset sounds and the other one always eats rhyme sounds. Using common words the students say what sounds each puppet eats. At the most difficult level, students match onsets and rhymes from sets of three (For example, "This mitten says s. Here are three mittens, this mitten says *push*, this one says *last* and this one says *sing*. Which mitten goes with s?"). As in earlier modules, students are also given opportunities to create their own exemplars in many of the activities and share these with their classmates.

Module 5: Shapes, Colors, and Letters

In this module, the focus is on the rapid naming of shapes, colors, objects, and letters. The student's task is to identify and name a series of shapes, colors, and letters. Students complete a range of tasks with shapes first, followed by colors, colored shapes, and finally with letters. For example, students are first shown a series of five common shapes and asked to identify them. The level of difficulty is increased by having children first identify one shape, then two, then three, and so on. Students are then shown a single row of shapes and asked to name them as quickly as possible. The level of difficulty is increased by adding rows, until students are naming five rows of shapes. This procedure is repeated for colors, colored shapes, and letters. Again, students create their own exemplars when completing these activities and share these with their classmates.

  In the next chapter you will find a discussion on trying out COGENT in a classroom and some evidence for its success.

COGENT Tasks in Pictures

Module 1: Squeeze and Say

- Language starts as instruction from outside then it becomes internalized.
- The child attends to instruction from an outside agent
- The process of attention takes the form of two kinds of activity:
    1. movement
    2. orienting response or attention

Module 2: Clap and Listen

Some children may need planned experiences to develop auditory discrimination.

Phonological processing and working memory, together, are absolutely needed for preparing children to begin reading

Module 3: Funny Relatives

Understanding of syntax and comprehension

Comprehension depends on six important things:

- *Analyzing words phonologically*
- *A good working memory*
- *Inferencing*
- *Actively search for meaning*
- *Vocabulary*
- *General knowledge*

Module 4: Name Game

- Revisits phonological training.

- Onset and rhyme discrimination.

- Prepares for spelling.

Module 5: Shapes, Colors, and Letters

Rapid automatic naming of letters is the foundation.

Shapes and objects as well as naming colors are linked to naming letters and words

10

COGENT Works: Early Evidence

Das, Hayward, Samantaray, and Panda (2006) Study

This study, done in 2006, was the first pilot investigation of COGENT (Cognitive Enhancement Training). It was essentially a demonstration of the possibilities of the COGENT program when applied to a significantly disadvantaged group of children. Admittedly, we did not meet rigorous scientific criteria; however, the study gave us an opportunity to illustrate the appropriateness and efficacy of the program.

Three of the modules were administered to a group of 11 disadvantaged children, ranging in age from 4 to 7 years, living in an orphanage in India. Caregivers at the orphanage reported that these children exhibited academic, emotional, and attentional problems, and were considered most at risk for academic and reading failure. Pretests and posttests of reading and cognitive measures show that 88 percent of the children made modest gains in word reading in the posttest. The performance norms on this test were for American children whose mother tongue is English, whereas the children in the mentioned sample only spent approximately one hour daily learning English as a subject in school. We suggest that because the quality of schooling these children receive was not comparable to schooling available in North American schools, and because English was not spoken in the community in which the children lived, even these small gains in word reading were remarkable achievements.

The gains in the cognitive test scores were also encouraging, with 54 percent of children showing gains in all four cognitive processing domains on which they were tested. Thus, COGENT not only appeared to help the children with academic performance, but also helped them in many ways which were not reflected in the standardized tests. It was observed that all children responded positively to program activities and the interactive learning ambience.

Hayward, Das, and Janzen (2007) Study

This study was motivated by the challenge of improving the reading abilities of aboriginal children who have experienced several years of reading failure. Reading is probably the single most important skill that children need to succeed in our current educational system. Statistics reveal chronic school dropout rates among Aboriginal youth. While the reasons for such statistics are necessarily complex, one contributing factor to school failure is early reading failure and our education system's inability to properly identify and assist those with persistent reading disabilities. Aboriginal youth have reported that reading difficulties contributed to their decision to leave school.

We examined whether or not COGENT would result in significant improvements in reading abilities of children (2- to 3-year-olds) who had been failing in regular classroom reading programs. The children were Canadian First Nations (FN) children who had been identified as poor readers in Grade 3. We were most interested in the meaningful and practical reading outcomes from this study as they related to "bridging" or "narrowing" the gap between poor readers and their peers with an average reading ability.

Two classes of Grade 3 children were provided classroom intervention three times weekly, in 30 minute sessions with COGENT, over the school year (October to May). Accounting for school holidays and cultural and community events, a total of 30 hours of instruction was offered. One class had 11 students who were poor readers, while the other class had six children who were poor readers and had been diagnosed with having Fetal Alcohol Effects, Attention Deficit Hyperactivity Disorder (ADHD), Conduct Disorder, and so on. A "no-risk" control group consisted of two classes of students (n = 23) who did not need remedial work according to the school and should benefit adequately from classroom instruction. All children were tested on reading tasks in September, December, and May.

There were several educationally significant findings regarding bridging and narrowing the gap mentioned earlier for many children. Participation was seen to narrow the gap in both word reading and reading comprehension, and bridge the gap in decoding of pseudo-words, a noteworthy finding for FN children, who have been regarded as chronically poor readers.

When we examined individual child records, the performance following COGENT intervention exceeded our expectations for children with long-standing reading failure. We refer here to the ongoing concern that interventions only result in stabilization of reading deficits for children with long-standing reading disabilities. The study found that even the weakest readers gained from the COGENT intervention, as shown by a significant decrease in the number of children below the 5th and 10th percentiles. The majority of children were performing at or below these percentiles across all measures in the pretest. At the posttest stage there remained only two or three children at or below these percentiles.

On tracking the effect of treatment by calculating improvement rates per hour of instruction, we found that following both intervention periods, the benchmarks suggested by Torgesen (2002) were surpassed. These alternative methods of tracking improvement led us to suggest that the gap had been bridged for word decoding and narrowed in both word reading and reading comprehension. These are important findings, particularly related to word reading and passage comprehension, which have historically been the most difficult areas in which to effect change in children with long-standing reading failure. Given the population of children we worked with, where there is a history of poor school attendance, low motivation, and differing cultural experiences related to home literacy, these improvements have an added importance.

Snapshots of the COGENT study of First Nations (Canadian native) children

- Tested COGENT over a full school year.
- Grade 3 children with severe reading problems.
- One class also had children with multiple problems such as Fetal Alcohol Syndrome (FAS) and severe emotional/behavioral problems.
- Tested against a group of normally functioning children who got regular classroom instruction only.
- Pretested in fall, and administered posttest in January and in May/June.

Conclusions

- COGENT provided a means to improve reading in all areas (decoding, word reading, and comprehension).
- This improvement was significantly greater than a control group (relative to their starting point), so much so that many children were within the "normal" range of reading by the end of the remediation.
- The classroom-based administration had obvious advantages in terms of resources.
- Kids loved it, and teachers came to see how effective it was.
- The school saw huge improvements on the last year's provincial achievement testing, and a majority of children met provincial standards.
- Huge improvements were noted in written composition and comprehension.

Future directions

- There are still many things we need to learn about literacy among aboriginal learners.
- We need to start much earlier to prevent reading problems.

11

How does Reading Readiness Work?
A Taste of COGENT

COGENT is a cognitive and reading stimulation program. The program should benefit cognitive development, typically of developing children as well as children with special needs, such as those with limited exposure to literacy, mild developmental delay, language impairment, and children at risk for developing dyslexia and other learning difficulties. The program has been effective in skill-building, in preparation for reading in a clinical tutoring situation, as well as for small-group instruction. As discussed in the previous chapter, COGENT holds a great deal of promise as a remediation program for small classrooms.

COGENT is designed to provide alternative routes toward the development of reading and academic skills. The program is based on broad developmental theories, extremely important to cognitive and language development, while using basic cognitive processes described in PASS. It is intended for children aged four to seven, preschoolers to children in early school years, who need to be prepared for reading. However, some teachers are experimenting with it for even older children who appear to be resistant to acquiring prerequisite skills for reading. COGENT may prepare children for receiving PREP in case they still require reading intervention.

There are five modules that make up the COGENT program, as mentioned in the previous chapter.

1. Squeeze and Say
2. Clap and Listen

3. Funny Relatives
4. Name Game
5. Shapes, Colors, and Letters

A Student Activity Completion Checklist (SACC) is provided at the end of each module so that the student's progress may be tracked.

MODULE 1: Squeeze and Say

Attention is a problem with many preschool children, children with developmental delays or those from disadvantaged backgrounds. Another difficulty is learning to control and regulate one's own behavior using internal speech. During the development of this ability some children will have an external dialogue with themselves, for others the dialogue is internal, and for some children it may not be spoken even silently. To explain further, internal dialogue uses internal speech. The complete process of internalization may begin with silent speech, but some children may skip this stage. Internal speech, which is the child's own private way of speaking to him/herself, replaces external speech when children have gone further in their cognitive development. In normally developing children, this occurs around the age of five. For children with developmental delays or disadvantaged backgrounds, it may take longer.

The major challenge for many children is that their attention has to be mobilized and focused on relevant stimuli; they cannot afford to be distracted. If we can guide children to attend to the linguistic features of stimuli, along with training their attention, then we are achieving two things at the same time—improving their attention and enhancing their processing of language. Both of these skills are exemplified in Module 1.

The student's task is to either squeeze or not squeeze their hand in response to a series of pictures and directions presented by the facilitator. Pictures of animals and flowers are presented one at a time, in a variety of sequences. The student must squeeze his/her hand in response to an increasingly complex set of rules.

Levels of difficulty

Preliminary Tasks: Activities are provided so that students learn to discriminate and control their responses. First, students focus on increasing the speed at which they name common objects. Second, students learn to control their motor responses to visually presented stimuli (pictures of flowers and animals).

Difficulty Level 1: Consists of two parts; the first requiring only a motor response while the second a verbal and motor response.

Difficulty Level 2: Requires both a verbal and motor response while increasing the speed of responding.

Difficulty Level 3: Requires discriminating and processing an increased number of stimuli prior to responding.

MODULE 2: Clap and Listen

Children first learn words by listening to them. Auditory discrimination, that is, children's ability to tell two words apart when they sound almost the same (for example, *kate, gate*), requires the ability to discriminate sounds, also known as phonemes, and is learnt through day-to-day experience. However, some children may need planned experiences to develop auditory discrimination skills. In training children to do this, Module 2 activities draw children's attention to specific sounds in words and syllables. This is also referred to as phonological awareness, as children must attend to the sound structure of words in order to read. Attention to sounds in a word is enhanced when students are asked to say the word aloud.

Memory of sounds in a word or memory of words just spoken in conversation is as useful as discriminating words and sounds in words. In fact, children use many strategies for remembering words in conversation. For example, when listening to a sequence like "After you pick up the toys, I want you to put the big ones in the basket and small ones in the closet", some children may rememberer the sequence by repeating it under their breath, while other children may visualize the chain of actions. Rehearsal or repetition of words under one's breath requires that one first says the words to oneself, that is, to covertly pronounce them. The faster you can do this, the more words you can remember. Fast visualization, likewise, helps in keeping a series of objects or actions alive in working memory. Some of the items in Module 2 provide occasions for children to develop their own strategy to remember sequences of words and phonemes.

Phonological awareness and working memory are absolutely necessary for preparing children to begin reading; Module 2 includes training in both.

The student's task is to respond to, or say, a series of words or sounds. Students listen to a series of words and when they hear a word that is different from the rest of the sequence, they clap their hands.

The level of difficulty is increased by (a) making the word series longer, (b) presenting the series at a faster rate, (c) discriminating sounds, and (d) holding information in working memory while simultaneously processing the information.

Levels of difficulty

Preliminary Level: Picture and word stimuli are used to orient students to the module tasks prior to the remaining tasks, which are primarily presented orally.

Difficulty Level 1: Requires a motor response to hearing a different word in a series spoken by the facilitator.

Difficulty Level 2: Requires a motor response to hearing a different sound in a series spoken by the facilitator. Speed of responding is also increased.

Difficulty Level 3: Requires motor and verbal responses while processing and holding an increasing number of stimuli in working memory.

MODULE 3: Funny Relatives

The syntax of sentences such as *The child is playing with the ball* or *The dog is chasing the cat* describes actions and emphasizes a serial organization of behavior. These types of sentences are referred to as syntagmatic structures by Luria (1981), and are understood and used by children before complex language structures. Later, children begin to understand and use sentences that convey relationships and involve the mastery of complex, hierarchically structured aspects of language (for example, *Both the sun and moon are bright* or *The earth is round like a ball.*). Luria describes these types of structures as paradigmatic. Understanding and using syntagmatic and paradigmatic structures enables children to comprehend the speech of others and to compose and write their thoughts as they go through higher grades in elementary school. For example, understanding the meaning of the sentences in an arithmetic problem is very often a matter of understanding paradigmatic relationships. Consider sentences like "Which of the two lines is shorter?" or "If this flowerpot has four flowers and the other has six, then how many flowers do the two pots have altogether?"

Module 3 focuses on comprehending sentence structure. Comprehension depends on several important aspects and therefore, should be encouraged. (All of these have been included to a certain extent for training in Module 3.)

- Analyzing words phonologically.
- Enhancing working-memory capacity.
- Inferring what is going to happen next and why, while listening to a conversation or a story.
- Actively searching for meaning—what is the general idea that's being expressed and how well is it getting across?
- Building vocabulary.
- Enhancing general knowledge of the subject matter, of the conversation, or narrative support, and increasing "knowledge of the world".

The student's task is to indicate the relationships described by the facilitator.

Levels of difficulty

Difficulty Level 1: Involves students placing objects in relation to each other, in response to verbal prompts provided by the facilitator.

Difficulty Level 2: Student places animals in an arrangement prompted by the verbalizations of the facilitator and verbalizes the spatial relationship. The student also responds to simple questions about the arrangement.

Difficulty Level 3: Consists of several tasks: (*a*) comprehension of short stories and construction of creative narratives, (*b*) understanding of adjectives, prepositions, and temporal relationships, and (*c*) increasing verbal working memory by remembering and applying inclusion and exclusion rules when naming objects, letters, and words.

MODULE 4: Name Game

The sound structure of words guides children's reading and spelling ability. Words are spelled as a whole or alternatively as a string of letters that require sounding out. New spellings are often learnt by analogy. For example, adding *ed to perform* spells *performed*. Add *ed* to *skid* and what do you get? A new spelling can also be learnt when the child knows the meaning of the word. For example, a child could tell the spelling of the word *ground* by connecting it with *grind* or with the solid ground on which you stand. *Human* connects with *man*, so a child who understands *man* will find it easier to spell *human*.

In spelling and writing, the successive position of letters has to be remembered, especially when the word is a long one. This requires use of working memory, that is, the child's ability to carry things in the head until the task is completed, in this case spelling a word. Sometimes, a child may be able to spell a word aloud but may make mistakes in putting it down on paper. Writing, then, requires a double dose of successive processing. This module focuses on successive processing abilities and revisits phonological awareness training, with onset/rhyme discrimination and sound blending/deletion tasks, which prepare children for spelling.

Levels of difficulty

Difficulty Level 1: Requires a motor or verbal response to hearing beginning sounds in words.

Difficulty Level 2: Requires (*a*) a motor and verbal response to hearing segments of words that are divided into onsets and rhymes, and (*b*) sound blending and deletion of compound words.

Difficulty Level 3: At this level students (*a*) say and read words, dividing them into onsets and rhymes, (*b*) say words using sound blending and deletion rules with one and two syllable words, and (*c*) apply inclusion and exclusion rules when naming words.

MODULE 5: Shapes, Colors, and Letters

Children generally learn to read words in the first year of school, although many children know the letters of the alphabet in kindergarten. Letters have to be recognized quickly in order to read words quickly. Those children who have mastered alphabet recognition well before they begin reading in Grade 1 have a vast advantage over those who have not. In fact, they turn out to be better readers even in Grades 3 and 4. In contrast, poor readers in those grades start off with a handicap; they are slow in recognizing letters of the alphabet. There are many reasons why some children are slow, and the absence of an environment of literacy at home, before they start school, is a major one.

Can we help children recognize letters quickly so that it becomes an automatic skill? To a great extent we can. The ability to rapidly name letters is the foundational skill that is linked to learning the sounds of words and translating spelling to speech, a skill that children must learn beyond kindergarten.

We also know that naming shapes, objects, and colors is linked to naming letters and words—children who are terribly slow in naming the former are likely to be slow in learning to rapidly name letters and words. Given that, we should include them in training programs for young children, especially those children who might be missing out on learning such skills at home and do not have much of an environment of literacy. Additionally, older children with developmental delays, dyslexia, or general reading difficulties would also benefit from such training.

Levels of difficulty

Preliminary Level: Focus the student's awareness on semantic features that will be used in later activities to improve speed, automaticity, and working memory capacity.

Difficulty Level 1: Focus on students identifying or naming a single feature (for example, color, shape, single letter).

Difficulty Level 2: Focus on increasing the speed and number of items that the students name, these items being still within a single feature (for example, color or shape).

Difficulty Level 3: Focus on increasing the speed and number of items, and get students to name items consisting of two features (for example, color and shape).

12

PREP: A Remediation Program Based on PASS

The PASS Reading Enhancement Program (PREP) is a remedial program for primary school-aged children who are experiencing difficulties with reading, spelling, and comprehension. It is based on the PASS theory of intelligence and should be understood within the framework provided by the PASS theory (see Chapter 4).

The training tasks in PREP are aimed at improving the information-processing strategies that underlie reading, namely, simultaneous and successive processing, while avoiding the direct teaching of word-reading skills.

Attention and planning are important aspects of the program. Specifically, attention is required to perform each task, and planning skills are developed by encouraging the children to discuss their strategies and solutions both during and following the tasks.

Strategies such as rehearsal, categorization, monitoring of performance, prediction, revision of prediction, sounding, and sound blending are integral parts of each task. Thus, by working through the tasks, children develop their ability to use these strategies. Rather than being explicitly taught, the children are encouraged to become aware of their use of strategies through a discussion of what they are doing. Growth in ability to use the strategies and awareness of appropriate opportunities for use are expected to develop over the course of the remediation.

The Structure and Content of PREP

The program in its recently published edition consists of eight tasks which vary considerably in content and in what they require of the child. Each task involves both a global training component and a curriculum-related bridging component. The global component consists of structured nonreading tasks that require the application of simultaneous or successive strategies. These tasks also provide children with the opportunity to internalize strategies in their own way, thus facilitating transfer (Das, Mishra, and Pool, 1995). The bridging component involves the same cognitive demands as its global component, and provides training in simultaneous and successive processing strategies that are closely linked to reading and spelling (Das, Naglieri, and Kirby, 1994).

The global tasks begin with content that is familiar and non-threatening so that strategy acquisition occurs in small stages (Das, Naglieri, and Kirby, 1994). Complexity is introduced gradually and only after a return to easier content. Through verbal mediation, which occurs through a discussion of specific strategies used, the children are encouraged to apply their chosen strategies to academic tasks such as word decoding. The global and bridging components are further divided into three levels of difficulty. This allows the child to progress in strategy development and, for those who already have some successful processing strategies in place, to begin at an appropriate level.

A system of prompts is also integrated into each global and bridging component. The prompts support and guide the child to ensure that he/she completes the tasks successfully with minimal assistance. A record of these prompts provides a monitoring system for teachers/facilitators to determine when the material is too difficult for the child or alternatively when the child is ready to progress to a more advanced level. If the child does not complete at least 80 percent of the tasks successfully, an alternative set of tasks at the same difficulty level is used to provide the additional training required.

Who is Most Likely to Benefit from PREP?

As discussed in the preceding chapters, a number of children who are highly motivated, emotionally well adjusted, and who have a supportive family environment, nonetheless experience reading difficulties. Broadly speaking, these children can be classified into two groups. The groups are similar, as children in both are unable to read at the level expected for their grade. The larger group comprises of children whose reading difficulties arise from a wide array of weaknesses in cognitive functioning, while children in the smaller group can be classified as dyslexic readers. How do we know, to which of the two groups a child belongs? The poor reader from the larger category is likely to struggle in other subjects that do not require a lot of reading, and may perform poorly on a wide variety of intellectual tasks. By contrast, the dyslexic child has specific cognitive processing difficulties that are related to converting spelling to speech, that is, phonological coding (see Chapter 4). Both types can benefit from PREP, but for children with attention deficit and/or severe difficulties in planning, PREP will only be effective if supplemented by appropriate treatment programs.

How does the PASS Model Apply to Reading Skills?

Kirby and Williams (1991) argue that the cognitive processing associated with reading passes through eight distinct and increasingly complex levels of abstractions: (a) features (components of letters), (b) letters, (c) sound or syllable units, (d) words, (e) phrases, (f) ideas, (g) main ideas, and (h) themes. At each level, items of information are recognized (simultaneous processing) and ordered (successive processing). In other words, both simultaneous and successive processing are required at each level.

1. Each letter consists of various features—vertical, horizontal or oblique lines, and semicircles.
2. The letter has to be recognized as a whole after its components have been put together successively. Uppercase letters (A, B) have to be distinguished from lowercase letters (a, b), yet the child must recognize that A = a, B = b. Thus, simultaneous processing is also required.
3. The various sounds of letters, especially vowels, have to be distinguished (simultaneous processing) and put together serially.
4. Words must then be read, either as whole patterns or as strings of phonemes (when the words are long or unfamiliar).

5. Meaning must be obtained from phrases; it is not enough to know the meaning of each individual word in phrases like *hot-headed comment* or *bone-chilling cold*. We need to understand their meaning in the context of other words in the phrase, and this requires both processes.
6. The ideas represented by words, phrases, and sentences need to be understood.
7. The ideas need to be sorted into main and secondary ideas. For example, what is the main idea in the sentence *While walking on ice, he fell through it?*
8. Finally, themes have to be identified in order to make sentences, paragraphs, and the entire text meaningful. "In small proportions we just beauties see", when combined with "In short measures life may perfect be", gives the reader a theme to understand the two sentences. Simultaneous and successive processing are both needed for comprehension, as are attention to the sequence and combination of words, and a plan to extract the meaning of the lines. Moreover, if the child does not have an adequate knowledge base, he or she may read the poem and understand each word but still miss its meaning.

In the case of a child who fails to learn to read, the failure is primarily due to a problem with successive processing, that is, the process that helps the child to sequence different items, letters, or words. A child cannot read if he/she cannot remember the exact sequence of letters in each word and then convert these words into speech. Thus, difficulties in successive processing may cause difficulties in acquiring and/or using phonological coding, which may, in turn, lead to reading failure.

On the other hand, when a child can read but struggles to understand what he or she is reading, the difficulty probably stems from weaknesses in simultaneous processing. Comprehension as an aspect of reading is very different from basic word decoding and is also more difficult to remediate.

' The PREP approach seeks to identify the most important processing needs of the child and to concentrate remediation in those areas.

Thus, a PREP facilitator will focus on successive processing to develop decoding skills or, alternatively, focus on simultaneous processing to develop comprehension.

It is important to note, however, that no cognitive task requires one process alone. It is a matter of emphasis. Depending on the task requirements and individual preference, the child may focus most strongly on one of the processes.

To sum up, then, PREP provides:

- alternatives for children who cannot use simultaneous or successive processes well,
- experience and practice for children who have not developed simultaneous or successive processes, and
- specific training in recognizing which method is most efficient for a given task (Kirby and Williams, 1991).

How Different is PREP from Phonetics Instruction?

Every child tries to learn to read in the first year in school. Indeed, it is no surprise that a few do not, or cannot, learn from instruction in reading. We are surprised that almost all children learn to read in the first year. There are many conditions that help children to read—instruction and some kind of blueprint in the child's brain are the two most important conditions that help the child. But when children fail to learn how to read, remediation becomes necessary. As said before, remediation begins when instruction fails.

Many attempts at remediation have been made using phonetics training and methods of teaching phonological coding. One of the well-known training studies was carried out by Lundberg, Frost, and Petersen (1988). While reading a brief summary of this study, be aware that they were training normal children to read, and did not select dyslexics or particularly poor readers. We suggest that the PREP program is very different from a phonological coding training program; it goes beyond phonological coding. Rather, it combines a general training of PASS processing with curriculum-related remedial training that is derived from the PASS theory. The PASS approach to reading disability is different; those who would not normally improve with phonetics instruction are to be trained both in basic cognitive processes as well as in curriculum-related tasks that replicate these processes.

In their classic article on effects of phonological training on 235 preschool children, the authors report a longitudinal study. The children had daily training session over a period of eight months and were compared with 155 children who did not receive this training. Effects of the training on children's progress in reading and spelling were tested in first and second grades. The program was like a game. First, a period of rhyming games using nursery rhymes, then later, segmentation of sentences into word units and exercises that made the children aware of the length of words and improve their knowledge of syllables. In the third month of the program, phonemes were introduced. But to make the task easy for the children, the word *Tom*, for example, was uttered by the examiner as *t-t-t-t-om*, *Tom*. As discussed in Chapter 2, phonemic awareness tasks such as initial phoneme identification, phoneme segmentation, and phoneme synthesis were used. The authors discussed the results and concluded that the development of rhyming ability does not seem to be strongly dependent on formal training. What is rhyming? It is sensitivity to sound similarity, and it seems to develop naturally through the experience of the child. We have also discussed in a previous chapter that training in rhyming alone does not improve word reading among those who are developing a reading disability; it has to be combined with spelling that hastens growth in reading ability in children entering the alphabetic stage. Awareness of syllables is more natural and accessible as compared to phonemes.

Lundberg, Frost, and Petersen suggest that this is so because in order to attend to syllables the child does not have to ignore the natural unity of the articulatory act. Phoneme segmentation, like initial phoneme recognition, is not naturally acquired. Therefore, extra training given to the children in the training group made them gain superior skills in phoneme segmentation.

In this widely quoted paper, the sample was different from the sample chosen in our own studies. This was an unselected group of children who had no obvious measures of reading difficulties.

Also, the type of training that was given, that is, phonemic segmentation, initial phoneme identification, and so on, obviously focused on phonemic awareness but not on the cognitive processes that might underlie phonemic awareness.

This is different in our research on PREP, which is presented in the next section, where the underlying processes were emphasized.

Shape Designs (presented in the next chapter) is one of the PREP tasks that may improve comprehension. In the meanwhile, let us take a look at the research that shows the effectiveness of PREP.

PREP and Its Efficacy: A Timely Summary

PREP was originally designed to be used with students in Grades 2 or 3. In the present study, summarized here, eight tasks from PREP were selected and adapted for the Grade 1 level.

Das, Mishra, and Pool (1995) used PREP with a group of 51 Grades 3 and 4 students with reading disabilities, who exhibited delays of at least 12 months on either the *Word Identification* or *Word Attack* subtest of the Woodcock Reading Mastery Test-Revised (WRMT-R). Participants were first divided into two groups—PREP remediation and a no-intervention control group. The PREP group received 15 sessions of training, in teams of two students each, over a period of two-and-a-half months. Children in the control group participated in regular classroom activities. After the intervention, both groups were tested again, using the Word Identification and Word Attack subtests. The results indicated that while both groups gained during the intervention period, the PREP group gained significantly more on both Word Identification and Word Attack subtests.

Carlson and Das (1997) report on two studies using a small-group version of the PREP for underachieving Grade 4 students in Chapter 1 programs. (Chapter 1 is a classification used in California for poor readers who have no mental retardation.) In the first study, the experimental group received 15 hours of "add-on" training with PREP, over an eight-week period. Both the PREP and control groups (22 and 15 students, respectively) continued to participate in the regular Chapter 1 program. Word Attack and Word Identification subtests of the WRMT-R were administered at the beginning and the end of the study. The results showed significant improvement after training in PREP as well as significant group–time interaction effects. The second study essentially replicated these results with a larger sample of Grade 4 students. Since then, several other replication studies completed in the same school district have essentially reproduced the original results with children from Grades 3, 4, 5, and 6, and with both bilingual (Spanish–English) and monolingual (English) children.

The effectiveness of a modified PREP (for an older group) was studied by Boden and Kirby (1995). A group of Grades 5 and 6 students, who were identified a year earlier as poor readers, were randomly assigned to either a control or an experimental group. The control group received regular classroom instruction and the experimental group received PREP, in teams of four students, for approximately 14 hours. As in previous studies, the results showed differences between the control and PREP groups on the Word Identification and Word Attack subtests. In relation to the previous year's reading scores, the PREP group performed significantly better than the control group. Finally, the study by Parrila, Das, Kendrick, Papadopoulos, and Kirby (1999) is an extension of the these experiments but with three important changes: (a) the control condition was a competing program given to a carefully matched group of children; (b) the participants were beginning readers in Grade 1 and therefore younger than the Grade 3 to Grade 6 participants in the previous studies; and (c) the training was shorter in duration than most of the previous studies. The more stringent control condition was seen as an important test of the efficacy of PREP. The study attempts to demonstrate the efficacy of PREP by showing its advantage over a meaning-based reading program received by the control group.

Fifty-eight Grade 1 children experiencing reading difficulties were divided into two matched remediation groups—PREP and meaning-based. Results showed a significant improvement in reading ability (Word identification and Word Attack) for the PREP group, and the gain was larger than it was for the meaning-based training group. Relevance of the children's CAS profile was demonstrated as follows. Further results indicated that the high gainers in the PREP group were those with a higher level of successive processing at the beginning of the program. In contrast, high gainers in the meaning-based program were characterized by a higher level of planning.

Taken together, these studies make a clear case for the effectiveness of PREP in remediating deficient reading skills during the elementary school years. The studies described indicate that word decoding improved after completion of PREP. These results suggest that PREP is effective with elementary school students who have reading and decoding problems that are related to successive processing difficulties. PREP's success in Spain and South Africa also indicates that the program can be effectively adapted to various cultural contexts.

PREP and Current Educational Theory

Cognitive process-based training, such as PREP, has gained widespread academic credibility as an example of applied cognitive psychology. In this context, a new textbook by Ashman and Conway (1997) makes a significant contribution to educational theory.

A number of process-based training programs are now available to remedial teachers. Unlike PREP, however, many of these have not been tested in controlled experiments, nor has their effectiveness been clearly linked to a theory. Schools, teachers, and parents should be careful to select a program based on a clear and consistent theory, whose effectiveness has been validated by independent scientific studies.

PREP in the Classroom

PREP is meant to complement, not replace, regular classroom instruction. It is primarily not designed for large classroom application. It is one of the best programs available for hard-to-teach poor readers in very small groups because

1. it aims at reducing the specific deficit in the child's cognitive functions;

2. it can do that only when each child has the opportunity to develop his/her own strategies; and

3. it provides optimal conditions for adult–child interaction.

However, PREP, particularly with regard to its global tasks, can be used in large classroom-size groups for cognitive stimulation. This will promote the development of strategies that are fundamental for reading and thinking in kindergarten as well as primary school. It can also be helpful in providing the appropriate cognitive framework for children in homes and communities that lack a literate environment.

Das, Mishra, and Pool (1995) suggest that training in simultaneous and successive processing, for children in kindergarten to first grade who have not yet learned to read, may prevent the later development of reading difficulties. A *Professor PREP Junior Series* has been designed with simplified PREP tasks that can be used as cognitive enrichment activities for young children.

Review of the PASS Diagram

The PASS processing model has been discussed in previous chapters, particularly in Chapter 4. The PASS model diagram has been presented earlier (see Figure 4.2) for quick reference, as the examiner sets out to implement PREP.

We should remember when applying PREP training that poor reading can be a combination of all of the PASS components—input, PASS processing difficulties, inadequate knowledge base, and the requirements of output.

Input

Concurrent—together, all at once

Sequential—one after another

- Does the child prefer one to the other?

Processing

Arousal-Attention

- Is the person alert?
- Is the person motivated?
- Can you bring the task to be the focus of the person's attention?
- Can the person resist distractions?
- Can you prevent external inhibition (reduce distracting factors in the environment)?

Coding

Simultaneous and Successive

- Which part of the task requires simultaneous processing? Which part requires successive processing?
- Can you detect the relative weakness of the person in one of the processes?
- Can you, then, modify the task to suit the person?
- Suppose it is an arithmetic problem—reading and comprehension are required—and the person is poor in simultaneous processing. How will you help?

Planning

Strategies for attending to, and coding information. **Evaluation** of feedback and thinking ahead.

- Can the person practise some parts of the task until these become automatic? This will reduce the load on planning.
- Everyday activities require judgments and decisions. Can you identify the critical parts, and check if the person does these automatically, and, if not, which parts need deliberate planning by the person?

Output

Motor Program for Output

- Does the task require a great deal of motor programming (handwriting)?
- Does the person need help? ("I understand I am asked to take down dictation, but I cannot hold the pencil properly and cannot write fast. What do I do?" It is a combination of simultaneous and successive aspects of the motor program.)

Execution of action

Motor

- Can the person do the task physically? (Coordination and movement)

Speech

- Can the person articulate clearly in response to your tasks? (For example, "Tell me the words you just read.")

Knowledge-base

Experiential

- What part of the task requires mostly experiential knowledge?
- Can you assume that the person had the right opportunities for acquiring it? (Color of apples and oranges, shape of a baby-carriage, names of the pictures, such as jug, spout, bug, in a vocabulary and writing test.)

Formal

- Does the person have adequate training? (Knows all the letters of the alphabet; knows that English is read from left to right.)

13

A Taste of PREP in Words and Pictures

The eight tasks that comprise PREP are—window sequencing; connecting letters; joining shapes; transportation matrices; related memory; tracking; shape design; and shapes and objects. A brief description of these tasks follows.

Window Sequencing

Global

This task focuses on successive processing. The student is asked to reproduce the order of a series of chips that vary in color and shape, in the same order in which they are presented by the facilitator. The chips are presented one at a time, left to right, through a small window. Each chip appears in the window for about a second. The series range in length from three to six chips. Four series of each length are presented per session, for a total of 12 items.

There are three levels of difficulty in the task.

- *Difficulty Level 1*: Involves sequences of two different types of chips (circles and squares) while the color remains constant.
- *Difficulty Level 2*: Involves different color chips (white, yellow, blue, and black) while the shape remains constant.
- *Difficulty Level 3*: Involves manipulation of both color and shape of the chips.

Bridging

The student's task is to (a) reproduce a series of letters in the same order in which they are presented by the facilitator, and (b) say or write the word that is spelled by the letters. The letters, which the student views for approximately one second through a window, are presented one at a time or in consonant or vowel combinations. There are three levels of difficulty which correspond to the phonetic complexity of the words used.

Connecting Letters

Global

The student is required to follow a line to find which letter on the left side of a card is connected to which letter on the right side of the card. Each card contains five letters on each side. The students are presented with each item individually. They are then required to write (or say) all of the connections. After an initial trial, the facilitator directs the student's attention to any errors so that corrections can be made.

There are three levels of difficulty (three items are presented at one difficulty level during a single session).

- *Difficulty Level 1*: Contains strings that are color-coded to aid in scanning.
- *Difficulty Level 2*: Contains black lines only.
- *Difficulty Level 3*: Contains black lines as well as "distractor" lines that are not connected to any letters.

Bridging

The student is presented a card with a column of five letters on the left side and a column of five letters on the right side of the page. The letters are connected with lines that run across the page. Along these lines there are more letters. Sometimes the letters are presented alone and sometimes they are in small groups (consonant or vowel blends, or digraphs). Together, the sequence of letters on each line forms a word. Each line is color-coded. The student is required to visually follow each line, mentally connecting the series of letters that run across the page, and say or write the word that is spelled by the letters. Four levels of difficulty are provided. Each corresponds to the phonetic complexity of the words.

Joining Shapes

Global

This task focuses on successive processing. The purpose of the task is to join a series of geometric shapes with a line in response to (*a*) a series of verbal instructions and (*b*) a set of rules provided by the facilitator. The shapes (triangles, squares, and hexagons) are presented in rows on a sheet of paper. Each row of triangles, squares, and hexagons is separated by a row of circles. In each session, six items with varying numbers of rows are presented. The first two items contain one row of triangles and one row of squares, with a row of circles in between. The third and fourth items contain one row of triangles, one row of squares, and one row of hexagons, with rows of circles in between. The fifth and sixth items contain a row of hexagons, a row of triangles, a row of squares, and another row of hexagons with rows of circles in between.

Bridging

Several rows of letters are presented to the student on a sheet of paper. The purpose of the task is to join the letters from the top row to the bottom row, moving diagonally from left to right, and following a set of rules to produce a word. When the student reaches the bottom, he/she takes the last letter of that word as the first letter of the next word and proceeds back to the top in the same manner to produce another word. This is continued until the student reaches the end of the sheet. The student is required to tell the facilitator the words that he/she formed. There are four levels of difficulty, corresponding to the length of the words.

Transportation Matrices

Global

The student's task is to reproduce a series of transportation pictures in the order in which they are presented. The entire sequence is shown for approximately five seconds and then turned over. Then, moving from the student's left to right, each individual picture is displayed for approximately two to three seconds and then turned over again.

Bridging

The student's task is to reproduce a series of letters in the correct order and state the word that is formed by the letters. The letters are exposed on a single line matrix which is divided into cells to match the number of letters in the word. The letters are presented simultaneously, and then one at a time, in their respective cells in the matrix, using a window shield. There are four levels of difficulty, corresponding to the phonetic complexity of the words.

Related Memory

Global

This task involves both simultaneous and successive processing. The student's task is to match the front half of an animal with its appropriate other half. Three front halves are presented in a column on the left side of a page and one back half is presented on a card that is placed on the right side of the page. The student is required to make a verbal prediction about which front and back half go together. Once he or she has done so, they place the front and back half together to determine whether the response was correct. The student is then allowed to alter his/her prediction, if necessary. There are three levels of difficulty, corresponding to the degree of discrimination required.

Bridging

The purpose of this task is to (*a*) choose the proper front half of a word to match the other half and (*b*) to read the word. The student chooses from three front portions of words, which are placed on the left side of a page in a column. To the right of this column is the other half of one of the words. The student is required to draw a line between one of the front halves and the back half. There are four levels of difficulty, corresponding to the complexity of the words.

Tracking

Global

In the global part of this simultaneous processing task, the student is presented with a village map with houses and trees, and tracking cards that illustrate a path from a starting point to either a numbered house (Level 1) or a lettered tree (Level 2). The tracking cards outline the roads and street intersections on the map. The student's task is to survey each card and the map, and then locate the number of the house or the letter of the tree on the map.

The second version of this task involves a letter map (Tracking Map II) and tracking cards with squares identified by a letter of the alphabet. The student's task is to locate the appropriate lettered square.

Bridging

The student is presented with a map of the West Edmonton mall, on which several key features are identified: Shark World, Water Park, Bingo, Ice Palace, Miniature Golf, Submarine, Roller Coaster, and Water Slides. He/she is allowed some time to become familiar with the locations of these features. The student is then given a series of printed passages (eight in total), one at a time. Each passage specifies a point of departure and two to four key features (listed randomly in the passage) that are to be visited by the student.

The student's task is to

1. read each passage as it is presented (with as much assistance as is required),
2. identify the point of departure and the key features that are to be incorporated into the visit, and
3. use the floor plan (map) to trace a path that will begin at the designated point of departure, incorporate all the specified features, and move through the mall as quickly as he/she can.

The student begins with a passage that specifies two key features (including the point of departure) and finishes with a passage that specifies four features.

Shape Design

Global

This is predominantly a simultaneous processing task in which the student is required to (a) study a design that is presented for 10 seconds and (b) reproduce it with the colored shapes provided. The shapes include circles, rectangles, squares, and triangles, in three colors (red, blue, and yellow) and two sizes. The designs range from a simple combination of three shapes, different only in color, to a complex combination of six shapes, differing in color, shape, and size. The task is divided into three difficulty levels with six items at each level.

Bridging

The student's task is to read a phrase or story from a card that describes how two to five animals are arranged in relation to one another. He/she visualizes the scene with the animals appropriately positioned. Then, with the reading card turned over, the student arranges the animals to correspond with the scene as it was described in the phrase or story. There are three difficulty levels, corresponding to the number and complexity of relationships.

Shapes and Objects

Global

In this simultaneous processing task, the student is required to match a picture of an object to an abstract shape (Level 1) or match a colored chip (shape) to a geometric shape (Level 2). He or she is asked to sort the picture cards or chips into the shape category that each one most resembles. In Item 1, there are 15 individual cards which are matched to one of the three illustrated abstract shapes. For item 2, 24 colored chips are matched to one of the four illustrated geometric shapes.

Bridging

The student is presented with sets of 7, 10, or 13 phrases or sentences, subsets of which can be categorized on the basis of thematic similarity. These sets each contain either two subsets of three phrases, three subsets of three or four phrases/sentences, or four subsets of three phrases/sentences and a "distractor". The student begins with a two-group set, proceeds to a three-group set, and finishes with a four-group set. He or she is also presented with the appropriate number of labels, each of which identifies a thematic category. For each set of phrases/sentences, the student is required to

1. read the phrases/sentences aloud;
2. sort the items into the specified categories; and
3. identify the distractor.

14

Case Histories

A Teacher's Experience with PREP

From 1990 to 1998 I taught PREP to more than 500 students in the San Jacinto Valley of southern California, USA. This is a rural area which contains two Unified School Districts (Hemet and San Jacinto) with a combined elementary school population of 11,372 students, above-average teachers, and supportive parents.

All the students, from Grades 2 to 5, I worked with scored below the 35th percentile in reading on standardized achievement tests and, therefore, qualified for Chapter 1 remediation funding. Most of the Grade 4 students had "fallen through the cracks" and/or failed to improve their decoding skills in multiple programs since second grade. This was the main reason why both school districts were anxious to incorporate PREP into the curriculum. With this information in mind, I would like to describe how students improved and benefited from PREP.

Intervention was critical for these "at risk" students, and a classroom teacher with 30–35 students could not spare the time necessary for remediation. As Dr Jack McLaughlin, former Superintendent of the Hemet Unified School District, stated, "PREP works, it is cost-effective, straightforward to implement, and can significantly improve reading ability." The teachers were very cooperative about releasing students for one hour a day, four days a week, for eight weeks, in groups of six to 10. They were enthusiastic about the program from the start, for many reasons. The students showed an immediate growth in self-esteem and were more willing to try to read orally in the regular classroom. These factors improved the climate in the classroom. After the remediation was completed, it was not unusual for teachers to relate how much the students had enjoyed the tasks involved in PREP and how much overall improvement they had made in processing reading materials.

PREP caught the students' attention from the start. They came into the program stating that they hated reading (a normal reaction from children who cannot read), but soon came to class asking, "Which task are we going to do today?" The tasks were totally different from anything they had previously attempted. The nonverbal or "Global" section of each task is nonthreatening and allows all students to be successful, even those with limited English language skills. The benefit to the students is that this builds immediate confidence and sets the stage for a successful experience. The enthusiasm carries over into the more difficult "Bridging" section of each task, which deals with language.

Each task in the PREP program is varied, interesting, imaginative, and fun, which brings the students back for more. Because PREP is process-based rather than skills-based, the tasks offer a multitude of innovative ways to make learning exciting. For example, when we do the bridging tasks that present words, we define and discuss each word, and the students are asked to make up imaginative sentences using the word. Each student wants to make up a bigger and wilder story than the rest, and the enthusiasm is infectious. This, incidentally, helps tremendously with their ability to write sentences and paragraphs. Both teachers and students found this to be a beneficial by-product of PREP.

The simultaneous and successive processing skills learned during the eight weeks of remediation with PREP have improved the students' ability to decode reading material. Pretest and posttest scores over the last eight years corroborate this. In addition, the most amazing by-product of PREP is that by the end of the remediation period, the students had totally changed their minds about hating to read.

Comments from teachers

The following are few of the comments from teachers of two ISA schools following the PREP program on how the "hating to read" attitude changed.

- *Now willing to read orally.*
- *More fluent.*

- *Better comprehension.*
- *Word Attack skills are better.*
- *Volunteers to read in class.*
- *More confident.*
- *Likes to read to the class.*
- *Has shown great growth.*
- *Continues to be motivated to read.*
- *Attention span has shown some strengthening.*
- *Has an easier time decoding words.*
- *Much more fluent, seems more comfortable in oral reading.*
- *Shows more interest in wanting to read.*

Woodcock Reading Mastery Test was given before PREP (Pretest) and after PREP training (Posttest). The level of reading is reported according to expected level—Grade Equivalent readings are reported for four cases that follow. These have been reported by Catherine F. Longe, who is a PREP trainer from Hemer, California.

Robert J., fifth grade, age 11 years

Robert scored below the 35th percentile in reading on a standardized test. He was referred to PREP in spring because his teacher did not feel that his Word Attack skills were adequate to proceed to Grade 6 work in the fall. His mother did not agree with this evaluation because she felt that he had potential, even though he had to struggle with homework that involved reading. Robert had never read a book on his own. Halfway through the remediation program Mrs J. reported that Robert had brought a book home, read it, knew what he had read, and was excited about his accomplishment. In the classroom, Robert's Word Attack skills improved daily. Robert was promoted to the 6th grade (see Table 14.1).

Table 14.1 Woodcock Test Results-I

Pretest	Word Identification	4th grade	7th month
	Word Attack	3rd grade	4th month
Posttest	Word Identification	5th grade	1st month
	Word Attack	12th grade	7th month

Source: Report by Catherine Longe, PREP trainer.

Jorge A., fourth grade, age 10 years

Jorge scored at the 35th percentile in reading, on a standardized test. He was referred to PREP because he showed no interest in reading in class. He was very shy and spoke only Spanish at home and with his friends. As the remediation progressed he felt less threatened and became comfortable in the group of six students. The nonverbal global component of each task gave him the confidence to attack the bridging component, which involves the same cognitive skills. The "light" came on.

Jorge's parents would not allow him to borrow books from the library, in fear of the books being lost and them having to reimburse the school. Toward the end of the program, Jorge asked if he could borrow books from my classroom collection and joyously reported that he was reading to his younger siblings. Jorge is progressing well in class with a new feeling of self-confidence (see Table 14.2).

Table 14.2   Woodcock Test Results-II

Pretest	Word Identification	4th grade	2nd month
	Word Attack	5th grade	2nd month
Posttest	Word Identification	5th grade	3rd month
	Word Attack	9th grade	4th month

Source: Report by Catherine Longe, PREP trainer.

Kyle A., third grade, age 9 years

Kyle scored below the 35th percentile in reading, on a standardized test. He was referred to PREP because of his lack of reading skills, which held him back in all subject areas. He had a discipline problem and cried easily when asked to perform. Kyle was verbal and had a lot of general information from watching TV. Working with a group of children was difficult for him and he wanted to be the center of attention. A parent conference resulted in improved behavior.

Kyle had great difficulty with both successive and simultaneous processing tasks and gave up easily. As he gained strength in processing, his self-confidence also increased and he settled into working with the group. He found strength in his ability to use words imaginatively in sentences and was progressing in all areas at the end of eight weeks (see Table 14.3).

Table 14.3   Woodcock Test Results-III

Pretest	Word Identification	2nd grade	7th month
	Word Attack	2nd grade	9th month
Posttest	Word Identification	3rd grade	3rd month
	Word Attack	3rd grade	0 months

Source: Report by Catherine Longe, PREP trainer.

The recommendation was that the teacher's aide should continue working with Kyle on PREP tasks for the remainder of the school year. By the end of the school year, Kyle's teacher reported that he was "flourishing" in reading.

Francesca M., second grade, age 7 years

Francesca scored below the 35th percentile in reading, on a standardized test. She was referred to PREP in the fall because of low reading scores and academic immaturity. English was her home language but her working parents did not take the time to help her with homework or read to her.

The small group atmosphere gave Francesca the confidence to try. The variety of processing challenges interested her greatly and she never missed a session. The tasks were not easy for Francesca and she inspired others by her efforts. She was very good at figuring out workable strategies (see Table 14.4).

Table 14.4   Woodcock Test Results-IV

Pretest	Word Identification	1st grade	8th month
	Word Attack	2nd grade	5th month
Posttest	Word Identification	2nd grade	2nd month
	Word Attack	3rd grade	4th month

Source: Report by Catherine Longe, PREP trainer.

Francesca came up to grade level and discovered that she enjoyed reading after all.

It is interesting to note that in Francesca's case history, as in many others, the decoding skill that improved most significantly was the skill in reading pseudo-words or made-up words. This was particularly heartening because it indicates improved phonological awareness.

Anna and Alex: Two Grade 1 Children from Edmonton, Canada

Case study 1: Anna

Although PREP is typically recommended for 8- to 9-year-olds, this case history shows that it was effective for a 6-year-old who showed a specific weakness in successive processing.

Anna, aged six, received one-on-one remediation. Pre-intervention test results revealed that of the four cognitive areas assessed (planning, attention, simultaneous and successive processing), successive processing was her only area of weakness. On the two Woodcock subtests, she scored at the 12th percentile on Word Identification and at the 2nd percentile on Word Attack, indicating that at the time of pretesting, her reading ability was very weak. In addition, Anna's performance on the phonological processing tasks suggested that her phonetic awareness was very limited, prior to intervention.

Anna was friendly and extremely talkative throughout the remediation, but at times tended to be very distractible. At the start of the remediation she experienced very few difficulties in completing the global components of the successive tasks. The bridging components were more problematic, and Anna often required the highest level of prompting when reading words. By the sixth and seventh sessions, however, she was able to read most words with minimal or no prompting (prompting stages 1 and 2). It should also be noted that when she was able to apply her strategies successfully, her verbalizations of these strategies were excellent.

Simultaneous processing tasks were introduced during the eighth session, and Anna experienced no difficulties with either the global or bridging components. By the midpoint of the program she was independently reading most words from the preliminary level of the bridging tasks. With the introduction of the next level of difficulty, she continued to read most words without prompting. During the final sessions of the program, a marked improvement was noted in her ability to blend phonetic sounds. This improvement in Anna's word-reading ability was also reflected in her Word Identification and Word Attack scores, which were at the 23rd and 26th percentiles, respectively.

Case study 2: Alex

In the case of this 6-year-old, all four PASS processes were weak. Alex was one in a group of two students during the remediation process. He was weak in all four cognitive processing areas. His scores on the attention and successive processing tasks were particularly low. His scores on the Word Identification (<1st percentile) and Word Attack (2nd percentile) subtests of the WRMT-R were among the lowest in our sample. On the phonological processing tasks, his performance was also extremely weak (he scored zero on all three tasks), suggesting that he generally had a low mental ability.

Throughout the remediation process, Alex seemed to have difficulties in verbalizing his strategies. It was also often difficult for him to stay focused on tasks because he was very distractible. During the initial stages of the program some difficulties with the global components of the successive tasks were evident. Although, Alex appeared to have some strategies for completing these tasks (he was rarely able to verbalize these), he had difficulties in applying the strategies and the amount of prompting he required was often inconsistent. He was unable to complete the bridging components of these tasks without the highest level of prompting, and his knowledge of letter names and sounds was extremely limited. The global component of the Joining Shapes task (a successive processing task) presented particular problems for him, and his inability to consistently apply his strategies was especially evident. Alex also required a longer period of time than most other participants to complete this task.

By Session 7, some progress had been made on the bridging components of the successive tasks, and Alex was able to read a few of the words without the highest level of prompting. But any task that involved letters or words required additional time to complete. By the midpoint in the program (Session 9), however, he was able to complete most of the global components of the successive tasks with little or no prompting.

Alex also experienced considerable difficulties with the Tracking task. It is interesting to note that on a second simultaneous processing task (Shape Design) he was, nevertheless, able to complete five of the six items independently. During the final session, a marked improvement in his successive processing was evident in his ability to reproduce a series of six shapes (Window Sequencing—Global). This improvement, however, was not reflected in Alex's scores on Woodcock's reading tests, which remained unchanged from his pretest scores.

A Psychologist's Case

Significant reading gains after PREP intervention were seen in a child who experienced severe difficulties in reading and comprehension, and was described as suffering from attention deficit. This child received consistent training sessions, generally three times per week, using the PREP program. The child was evaluated at the age of 7 years and 1 month, and at 7 years and 5 months following the completion of the PREP training.

After each evaluation, there were significant gains on the previous evaluation on measures of reading and cognitive functioning. When first evaluated, at the age of 7 years and 1 month, prior to the intervention with PREP, his successive processing score was particularly low. When reassessed, following PREP, at the age of 7 years and 5 months, his scores had improved significantly in the areas of attention and successive processing. Scores on the two subtests of the Attention Processing Scale on the Cognitive Assessment System (CAS) revealed an improvement from high average/superior to very superior. Scores on the two subtests of the Successive Processing Scale on the CAS revealed an even greater increase, from below and low average to high and above average. His scaled scores on the CAS improved from one standard deviation to two standard deviations, a 14 percent to over 40 percent improvement, for the successive processing tasks. His performance on attention tests was at the high average range before intervention. Thus, he was definitely not suffering from attention deficit. Most probably, because of his severe difficulties in reading, he had developed into a restless and distracted child. His planning and simultaneous performances were above average from the beginning. Following PREP, his attention skills became even better and successive processing showed a phenomenal improvement.

Two subtests of WRMT-R (Word Identification and Word Attack) also revealed significant increases following the PREP training. Word Identification (read ordinary words) improved from a pre-training grade level of 2.0 to a post-training grade level of 4.1. Performance on the Word Attack subtest (reading made-up words, a good test of reading by sound) increased from a grade level of kindergarten to a grade level of 2.4, the appropriate level for his grade and age, following the PREP training.

The child's mother reported a significant improvement in her son's overall functioning. The reading improvement was confirmed by the child's teacher as well as through a special reeducation evaluation at his school.

Note: This case was provided by Martin Fletcher, a psychologist in Michigan, who specializes in cognitive training.

Two Mothers Speak

Forever in my heart

I remember so clearly, my daughter Sarah's first day of school. She was at last one of the big girls and was taking her first steps into the wonderful world of learning. On the way to school we talked about all the things she would do in the big school, the places she would go and see, and even what she wanted to be when she grew up. I was so proud of her maturity and eagerness to get on with the adventures of life. As she released her little hand from mine and kissed me goodbye, I realized that I was the one who didn't want to let go. At first I hesitated, but then stood back and looked at my little girl and then at her teacher and realized that I too was about to take a very big step in my life.

During the first few months, the joys and enthusiasm that once were became suddenly, for no reason I could explain, a living nightmare. My little girl, once so anxious and excited about growing up and going to school, became insecure, rebellious, and nervous. She hated school, she hated her teacher, she hated everything. She even hated me. Every morning when the alarm clock went off, I had to force myself out of bed, dreading the daily routine of constant excuses, fighting, yelling, and screaming just to get Sarah out of bed and ready for school. It was emotionally, mentally, and physically exhausting.

I spoke to Sarah's teacher and to other mothers. Maybe I was just overreacting and Sarah needed more time to settle down, they said. It would pass. Sarah's behavior was defined as "normal". But I, as Sarah's mother, had a gut feeling it was far more than that. Something was wrong, seriously wrong. And I was totally defenceless.

I have never compared any of my children to each other or to other children. I do not expect them to become a reflection of what I feel they should be or become; I see each of them as the unique individuals they are with their own wonderful characteristics, talents, and abilities. I simply love them for who and what they are, and the joy they bring into my life. But with Sarah, I started to notice that while other children in her class were progressing, she, despite all good intentions and efforts, wasn't coping. As each and every day passed, her frustration and anger became more apparent. I look back now and realize that Sarah knew she wasn't learning, but she didn't understand why. Worst of all, I didn't know how to help her. My gut feelings were dismissed simply because I was just her mother—what did I know?

Then I realized the problem was staring me in the face. One day when Sarah was reading her schoolbook to me, I realized something was seriously wrong. She wasn't reading—she was memorizing. She kept saying "Run, Jack, run", page after page, even with the book upside down. It didn't matter what page, what words— she had memorized the book perfectly. I couldn't believe what I was seeing. Sarah was compensating for her inability to understand what she was reading, and she was terrified she would get caught. So I skipped a page without her knowing but Sarah just kept saying "Run, Jack, run"—the page that she knew came next. When I attempted to explain to her that the words she was reading were wrong, she became angry and aggressive. So did I. What was happening to us was frightening. What was once dismissed as normal was now becoming an emotional snowball that I couldn't deal with, and neither could Sarah.

I was left no choice but to go at it alone. Sarah needed help and no matter what it took, I was determined she was going to get it. The pain was becoming unbearable and I simply couldn't take it any more—neither could Sarah. I decided to take her to a friend, Lesley Rosenthal, who is a remedial teacher, university lecturer, and educational psychologist. I asked Lesley if she would see Sarah and do her homework with her and assess her. I remember so clearly how scared I was. Was my child stupid, dumb? Would she never be able to read? Was I in fact just an overanxious, neurotic mother? Was all this happening because of me, I kept asking myself? I prepared myself for the worst.

I knew it wasn't going to be easy to get Sarah to agree to go either, so I disguised the assessment as play time with Lesley while I ran a few errands. The first visit was confirmed and the very next day I dropped Sarah off at Lesley's after school.

When I returned, Lesley explained that I was right about Sarah. She said that Sarah was not reading at her grade level, she was not coping, but that she knew why. Sarah was borderline dyslexic. Sarah wasn't stupid, she wasn't dumb: she had a learning problem, an invisible handicap. And I wasn't a neurotic mother either. I was immediately both relieved and frightened, as the next step was to discuss what could be done. I had heard horrific stories from other mothers that made me cringe, and what I expected was that this was now the beginning of a very long, emotionally draining journey that would last for years. Sarah would be dragged from therapist to therapist, program to program, until she just gave up on herself or until everybody just gave up on her. I wasn't prepared ever to do that.

Lesley highly recommended a program called PREP, the Pass Reading Enhancement Program, researched and developed by Dr J.P. Das. She recommended PREP twice a week for 30 minutes, and that Sarah should commence therapy immediately. When we left, I told Sarah that Lesley wanted her to come and play again. I told her that Lesley had told me that she had read to her and how impressed Lesley was and asked if she would like to go again. Without hesitation, Sarah agreed. But I was not prepared for the amazing stories I would hear and the changes that would take place over the next few weeks.

Sarah went to "play" with Lesley again the following week. Afterwards Lesley told me that first they had had to establish who was in charge. Sarah had insisted at first that she would play the teacher, but Lesley was adamant that she wanted to be the teacher. Finally, and with great reluctance, Sarah had agreed. In the car on the way home, Sarah made it clear that she wasn't too happy about this, but that she would discuss it with Lesley on her next visit as it was only fair that they took turns. I wanted to topple over in fits of laughter as I could just see my daughter negotiating who was in charge. There was no doubt she was her mother's child.

This was followed by several other sessions and after each one Sarah and I would discuss how the afternoon went. At first I wasn't too alarmed until it seemed that all Sarah was doing was playing with circles, squares, and triangles; cows, sheep, and horses; funny-looking shapes; animals cut in half; doing puzzles; drawing lines; playing the postman game; and putting cars, boats, tractors, and trucks and other pretty pictures of transportation in order. She described in detail how she had to show which shapes and letters Lesley had put in her window. I nearly fell over one day when Sarah informed me that she and Lesley would be going to the mall to shop on her next visit. Sarah, however, assured me that she didn't need any money.

I couldn't imagine how all this was helping Sarah to read. To make matters worse, all Sarah could talk about was playing PREP. She even insisted that she go to Lesley's house every day. In fact, the very moment Sarah arrived home from school she would phone Lesley to see if she could come and play. This was when I gave serious thought to approaching Lesley about my concerns and discussing with her the stories Sarah was telling me. While assuring her that I was aware that Sarah could exaggerate, I would tell her that I couldn't understand (if Sarah's stories were even half correct) what all this had to do with reading.

But my instincts told me to hold back. The change in Sarah was already obvious—she was again becoming the happy, delightful little girl I thought I had lost. As it turned out, I had made the right decision. When I investigated the PREP program and its theory, I learned that the games Sarah so often talked about were, to my fascination, specifically designed to provide a nonthreatening environment in which children could develop the internal strategies linked to reading, in their own way. It was so simple and so brilliant.

And so for the next eight weeks, for two afternoons a week, Sarah continued her PREP lessons: Eight weeks later, I had a completely different child. Not only was she reading at and above her level, she was reading everything she could get her hands on. She drove everybody crazy, especially her two brothers, 3 and 4 years older than she was, when she wanted to (and could!) read their books. She read every sign, every poster, every billboard. She read everything. When Sarah turned eight, she asked for a book, not a toy, for her birthday. Then she joined the library on her own initiative. It was one of the most exciting periods of my life. Even more incredible was the change I saw in my child, in how she learned to think in other areas as well. Not only did the PREP program develop her reading skills, I could also see how the life skills related to reading that she had acquired had a direct impact in improving her listening, planning, and organizational skills. Reading became, and still is today, an obsession with my daughter, and her new confidence has affected every other aspect of her life, socially and academically.

Now, every day as I sit with and watch my happy, confident, delightful little daughter read, read, read, I feel her grow closer and closer in my heart, where she will be for ever, right next to the PREP program.

Note: This testimony was provided by Kathryn M. Dudley from Johannesburg, South Africa.

We were all desperate...

My daughter Amy, who is currently attending fourth grade, has been in remedial reading since first grade. Throughout the years, I took her from one reading instructor to the other. She was in Kumon, a reading and math program, for about six months. She received 60 reading lessons through the Learning Success Center. I administered portions of the Phone-Graphics method five to six times a week for about 8 months. She also received Fast Forward at her school; this consists of approximately two hours of reading instruction per day, 5 days a week, for 10 weeks. She also went through Processing and Cognitive Enhancement Enrichment (30 sessions).

Besides this, I read about three or four preschool books to her at night when she was a toddler. We read together for 15 minutes a day, as requested by her teachers. I consulted with psychologists, reading specialists, teachers, and speech and language pathologists. I read books about reading and researched the library and the Internet.

All the reading programs she went through presented minimal improvement. She was reading by sight; she was never able to read a word that she had never seen before. Phoneme and syllable segmentation were poor. She was unable to blend sounds.

We were all desperate, when I saw a short description of the PREP program in the Riverside publishing catalogue. She had received half of the PREP, when the teacher wrote me a note telling me that she was very happy with Amy's reading improvement. I could not believe the teacher—I thought she was putting me on. I asked Amy to read a page out of the challenging books assigned for her to read. I could not believe her fluency!

Before the PREP, she would read the first two phonemes of a word and guess the rest. Because she has Attention Deficit Disorder (ADD), articles and pronouns are often missed when she reads. Amy is now reading, using sound blending, something she had never been able to do before. I was amazed at the amount of improvement after just half of the training. I can hardly wait for her to receive the rest.

I have told everyone I know about this reading program and they are all very eager to learn more about it. Amy's teacher is interested in having her daughter receive it because of the significant improvement in my daughter's reading. The PREP indirectly taught Amy strategies to use for reading; this is the way she is most likely to learn. I had noticed that she likes to learn using inductive strategies, but it was not until she received the PREP that this became even more noticeable.

I know other children can benefit from this innovative reading approach. I know it works and would recommend it, enthusiastically and with gratitude, for children struggling with learning to read.

Note: This testimony was provided by Enid Serrano Flaisher, a Speech and Language Pathologist from Michigan.

A School in Seattle

I am currently the reading specialist at Christ the King School in Seattle, Washington. I have been facilitating the Professor PREP program with nine students who are being pulled out of the regular classroom to receive specialised instruction because they are all performing below grade level. The students struggle in the areas of reading, writing, problem solving, and critical thinking skills. Five of the students are enrolled in the third grade and four are in the fifth grade. I administered the Woodcock Johnson Diagnostic Reading Battery test prior to the start of the program, and plan to administer the same test at the conclusion of the program in a couple of weeks from the time of writing. The purpose of the test was to see who would benefit from the program, by recognizing students who are at risk, and to measure the students' growth after participating in the program. I am anxious to see the results.

Throughout the past few weeks I have seen noticeable progress in several students' ability to verbalize the directions and strategy used in completing a given task of the program. They are also making progress in their ability to focus and listen for longer periods of time.

The Professor PREP program definitely captures the students' interest and provides a fun and successful learning experience. Students enjoy participating in the program. They seem to be responding well to it and, indeed, excelling. Motivating them to be pulled out of their regular classroom setting is easy because they enjoy the program and look forward to doing it. They find each task of the program different and challenging. One of my students commented that Professor PREP makes learning fun and is better than learning at a chalkboard. The learning manipulatives are great and hold the students' interest by making them active participants in the program.

Prior to this year the at-risk students participated in the Lightspan program, a curriculum-based educational software package. It was designed by educational experts to help students in kindergarten through sixth grade to build basic skills and to promote the development of critical thinking skills. After using both programs, I prefer Professor PREP. There is greater opportunity for developing higher-level thinking skills and for teacher–student interaction. I also feel that the Professor PREP program is easier to facilitate because students seem to enjoy and respond better to it than to others.

There are many strengths in the Professor PREP program. The manipulatives along with the ease of facilitating the program are two of its strengths. The administration manual is extremely user-friendly, while the small-group instruction allows many opportunities for student–teacher interaction. The program is designed to be used for many years. I believe the program was a wise investment and will help many struggling students to learn to read.

Note: This testimony was provided by Patricia Holcomb.

Some letters from PREP children in Patricia Holcomb's class

I think Professor PREP is fun because you learn words in a fun way. It helps me spell and sound out words. I can read better. I just stumble on some names and big long words.

Kirsten, 11, fifth grade

I like PP [Professor PREP] because it is helping me learn sounds and spelling, because it tells me words that I don't know. I like T-(transportation) cards because it helps me remember things. I like coming because it makes me listen better. I like PP because it is exciting because we play games. It is fun because we play. I like it so much. I feel I always want to come and play PP because it is a fun game to play because you learn more sounds.

Omna, 8, third grade

I like PP because it helps me learn sound and spelling so I can spell big words. I like the T-card because it help me memorize.

Stefan, 8, third grade

PP is making learning fun for me because it is easyer than lerning with a chalk bord. I like coming because I like to learn new things. Because learning is fun.

Blake, 8, third grade

PREP Impacts on Cognitive Processes: Summary of Case Reports

This summary shows the benefits of PREP training improvements not only occurred in reading, but also in some abilities for cognitive processing, especially in Successive processing (see Table 14.5). This process is associated with learning to read. These findings have been contributed by Dr Martin Fletcher.

Table 14.5   PREP and CAS Changes

Age (Yrs)	Test type	Planning	Simultaneous	Successive	Attention	CAS composite Score
9	Pretest	77	79	74	94	73
	Posttest	85	106	121	103	105
12.4	Pretest	85	115	91	105	99
	Posttest	91	126	106	114	113
13.2	Pretest	103	91	79	117	97
	Posttest	112	123	133	122	130
9.4	Pretest	81	102	88	98	89
	Posttest	92	116	102	94	101
12.5	Pretest	97	85	97	86	88
	Posttest	97	103	138	94	111

David's reading difficulties

David is a 12-year-old, right-handed child who is in Grade 7. His mother described him as a "fun" child who "asks wonderful questions and has a unique way of looking at the world". David was referred for an assessment due to concerns about his learning. Mrs J. indicated that David struggled with reading, math, and test-taking. She felt that David had above-average intelligence, as described in the following quote: "(David) is a bright, motivated child who struggles in school in spite of his intelligence." She reported that although David's grades were average, she found it difficult to watch David become more and more frustrated with school.

David attended a special education class for two hours per day, focusing on language arts; all other subjects were attended in a general education setting.

David's history is significant considering two incidents of head trauma, **one** occurring in September 2001, when David was 10 years and 5 months of age, and then another in September 2002, when David was 11 years and 5 months old. Both incidents were concussions that occurred while David was playing football.

Table 14.6 Wechsler Intelligence Scale for Children—Third Edition (WISC-III)

	Standard Score
Verbal IQ	105
Performance IQ	111
Full Scale IQ	112

Note: Mean = 100.

Table 14 .7 David's Pretest and Posttest Comparisons Following PREP

	Pretest		Posttest	
Subtest	Standard Score	Percentile	Standard Score	Percentile
Planning	71	3	94	34
Simultaneous	58	0.3	91	27
Attention	100	50	91	27
Successive	97	42	100	50
Full Scale	74	4	92	30

Table 14.8 Wechsler Individual Achievement Test-II (WIAT-II)

	Pretest		Posttest	
Subtest	Standard Score	Percentile	Standard Score	Percentile
Word Reading	77	6	92	30
Reading Comprehension	78	7	98	45
Pseudo-word Decoding	76	5	91	27

Tables 14.6 to 14.8 shows his test performance.

Six months following the completion of treatment, a follow-up call was made to Mrs J. Her comments are as follows:

David looked forward to the sessions. I see concrete evidence that he's improved. The stuff he learns at school now sticks better. His reading and writing are better; school has become easier. He's going out for the school basketball team ... this is something he wouldn't have done before. His confidence is so much better; it's such a relief! The change was more dramatic than I expected ... I wish I had known about your program earlier.

It is clear that the cognitive remediation program, PREP, was the intervention needed to help David strengthen his processing skills so that he could perform to his full potential—which he is now doing.

Conrad

Conrad is an 8-year-old, right-handed child who is in Grade 3. Conrad's mother accompanied him to the evaluation, and she provided historical information related to his development. She described her son as a "very loving" child who tends to need repeated directions to be able to complete tasks. This is creating problems both at school and at home. Conrad was referred for an assessment due to concerns about his learning. His mother indicated that Conrad was having problems staying on task and completing assignments.

At the time of the initial evaluation, Conrad was at risk of being permanently removed from his private school.

Table 14.9 Comprehensive Test of Phonological Processing (CTOPP): Composite

	Pretest	
	Standard Score	Percentile
Phonological Awareness	106	65
Phonological Memory	70	2
Rapid Naming	103	58

Table 14.10 Wechsler Individual Achievement Test—Second Edition (WIAT-II)

Subtest	Standard Score	Percentile
Word Reading	107	68
Pseudoword Decoding	112	79

It is worth mentioning that while Conrad's pretest scores were at the 10th percentile, or lower, for each of the four cognitive processing areas tested on the CAS, his scores on two of the three areas on the CTOPP and both of the areas on the WIAT were above the mean (50th percentile). This demonstrates the usefulness of CAS in assessing cognitive functioning, as it is not unusual for children who score at or above the mean on traditional standardized tests to, nonetheless, have a deficit in one or more areas of cognitive functioning. Till date, CAS is the only assessment instrument that measures these essential cognitive functions.

Table 14.11   Cognitive Assessment System (CAS) Results

Subtest	Pretest		Posttest	
	Standard Score	Percentile	Standard Score	Percentile
Planning	59	0.3	112	79
Simultaneous	61	0.5	112	79
Attention	71	3	112	79
Successive	81	10	111	77
Full Scale	55	0.1	116	86

The reason for Conrad's poor school performance was clearly his cognitive processing deficits. As shown earlier, Conrad's cognitive processing rose to the high average range in all areas. Follow-up calls to both Conrad's parents and school officials, which took place about 4 months following the completion of treatment, provided evidence that Conrad's scholastic performance had indeed improved. Conrad's mother and stepfather stated that "He's much more on-task than last (school) year. He's much more responsible and self-directed; he's always ready to go in the morning. I can see that his attention is much better. He's certainly not in danger of being kicked out of school!" A phone call to the principal of Conrad's school confirmed these statements. Mrs W. stated that the changes in Conrad's behavior and academic performance were "quite remarkable".

Two Case Studies from India

The following two case studies are from the Learning Clinic, run by the author, in Bhubaneswar, India.

Elisha Rout, 4th grade, age 9 years

Language of school instruction is English.
Mother tongue and majority language in the community is Oriya.

Elisha was reported by her teacher to be a poor performer in her class and was, therefore, tested for her intelligence and reading proficiency. She was found to be "average" in her overall intellectual functioning, planning, simultaneous processing, and attention, and "high average" in successive processing. When tested for reading proficiency, she was found to be at the level of 4.7 grade equivalent in word reading (Word Identification), but at the level of 2.4 grade equivalent in reading comprehension (Woodcock Reading Mastery Test norms). Elisha's problem, thus, was in comprehending the text, not in reading individual words comprising it. This could have affected her overall academic performance. She was given PREP instruction in a separate room at her school. Elisha was smart and sociable, and showed her willingness to join the program.

PREP tasks were chosen for Elisha keeping her requirement in view. Some of these were based on successive processing, but the majority focused on simultaneous processing. Elisha completed both the global and the bridging parts of the tasks based on successive processing without any difficulty and could read the words without any prompting. The task which focused on both simultaneous and successive processing (Transportation Matrices) was introduced in the 7th session (total 16 sessions). The global part and the bridging task I could be completed smoothly. But, bridging task II was difficult for her and she needed some prompting to complete the task. Following this, the tasks based on simultaneous processing were introduced one after another. Elisha could complete the global parts of these tasks with a little help. But the bridging tasks were difficult for her. Many words and concepts were new for her and she needed much prompting. However, her strategy to deal with the simultaneous processing problems developed gradually, which she verbalized with confidence towards the end of the program. The program was over in 16 sessions. By that time, she had started enjoying the tasks, particularly those involving animals and colorful pictures.

Ultimately, the improvement could be marked not only in Elisha's reading skill, but also in her cognitive functioning. In fact, she showed marked improvement in both word reading and reading comprehension, and jumped to the "superior" category in planning (CAS), in which she was "average" before remediation.

Table 14.12   Woodcock Reading Mastery Test (Grade Equivalent Scores)-I

Pretest	– Word Identification	4.7
	Passage Comprehension	2.7
Posttest	– Word Identification	8.7
	Passage Comprehension	4.9

Soumya Adyasha, 4th grade, age 9 years

Language of school instruction is English.
Mother tongue and majority language in the community is Oriya.

Soumya's academic performance was not good according to her teacher and parents. However, they reported her to be intelligent, but having no interest in studies. She was smart, talkative, and cheerful.

Soumya's pretest scores on tests of intelligence revealed her to be weak in simultaneous processing ("low average"), "average" in planning, attention, and overall intellectual functioning, and "superior" in successive processing. Her scores on the reading test suggested that she was at the level of 5.3 in word reading but more than a grade behind in reading comprehension. Soumya was referred to PREP.

Eight PREP tasks were chosen for Soumya, three of which focused on successive processing, four on simultaneous processing, and one on both. Soumya had no difficulty with the tasks based on successive processing, but she committed some spelling mistakes while writing down the words read by her. Soumya also enjoyed the task that focused on both simultaneous and successive processing, although its bridging task II was somewhat difficult for her. But she developed the strategy to complete the task following some prompting, and verbalized the strategies she was using very well. Soumya's problem, however, was her difficulty with completing the tasks focusing on simultaneous processing. The global parts of these tasks could be completed with no or little prompting, but in bridging parts of the tasks, she needed prompting (prompting stage 2), conceptual clarity, and assistance in understanding the meaning of difficult words. However, gradually, she felt the tasks to be easy as she could complete them successfully, developing appropriate strategies for the same, which she could even explain. The most important point was that she showed marked enthusiasm to come to the PREP sessions, taking interest in the tasks that involved colorful shapes, animals, and pictures; in fact, she became quite upset when the program came to an end. As Soumya herself reported, reading, by the time she completed the sessions, was no more a problem for her. The program was over in 16 sessions.

Somya's improvement in both reading and cognitive functions could be known from her posttest scores. She showed marked improvement in both word reading and reading comprehension, jumped from "low average" to "average" category in simultaneous processing, and "superior" to "very superior" category in successive processing, following remediation.

Table 14.13 Woodcock Reading Mastery Test (Grade Equivalent Scores)-II

Pretest	– Word Identification	5.3
	Passage Comprehension	3
Posttest	– Word Identification	11.3
	Passage Comprehension	4.6

Note: These cases were provided by Shamita Mohapatra.

III

The Next Steps

15

The Way Forward

We have discussed reading problems in this book under the three main themes of (*a*) assessment of reading ability; (*b*) identification of the cognitive deficit (in PASS processing) that is assessed to be causing any reading problem; and (*c*) remediation or prescription for the child who is struggling to read as a result of this cognitive weakness.

Together, these three aspects give us a better understanding of the difficulties experienced by children with dyslexia, and of the ways in which we can help them overcome their problems. It should be clear from the preceding chapters that the PREP remediation program is not a random collection of games and tasks, nor is it a drilling procedure or a more-of-the-same series of worksheets, but a rational program that is anchored in the PASS theory. We do not claim that PASS is a perfect theory or that PREP is a panacea or a magic bullet for curing dyslexia. However, PREP has achieved notable success with many children in countries around the world.

What are the Next Steps? Arithmetic Disability

Many children who are dyslexic also experience difficulties in arithmetic. This is partly because they struggle to read the arithmetic questions. In addition, however, some of them have comprehension problems, that is, even when the problem is read out to them, they cannot understand it. This indicates a deficit in simultaneous processing, the same cognitive process that is involved in word comprehension.

Comprehension is essential for problem solving in arithmetic; the child cannot choose the correct steps to find the solution unless he or she understands what the problem is. Another requirement for problem solving is planning. Because arithmetical computation has to be executed step-by-step, planning is required, first, to understand the link between the meaning of the problem and the steps that are necessary to solve it and, second, to execute those steps.

It is important, therefore, to distinguish between those whose main problem is comprehension and those whose main problem is planning. It should be mentioned that comprehension may be aided by presenting the problem in more than one way—for example, by using pictures and graphics in addition to explaining the problem in words.

Is it possible, then, to construct a program for boosting the planning process? Such a program would be linked to PREP, but its emphasis would be on planning and its prerequisite, that is, attention.

A beginning has been made (Naglieri and Das, 1997). The following research study was conducted by Naglieri and Gottling (1997). It used prompts and strategies to improve children's arithmetical problem-solving skills. Children who were weakest in planning were expected to benefit most from the training procedure, and that is exactly what the research showed.

Facilitating the Planning Process: A Study on Arithmetic Remediation

The relationship between planning and instruction was closely examined in a series of research papers beginning with Cromier, Carlson, and Das (1990) and Kar, Dash, Das, and Carlson (1992). The researchers developed a method that stimulated children's use of planning and had positive effects on their performance. This method was based on the assumption that the children's use of planning processes should be facilitated by prompts and by exposure to strategies rather than by direct instruction—the same assumption on which PREP is based.

These studies were used as a basis for two applied investigations by Naglieri and Gottling (1997) and also Naglieri and Johnson (2000). Both these investigations demonstrated that intervention designed to facilitate the use of planning significantly helped those with low initial scores in planning, but led to minimal improvement for those whose initial planning scores were high. This finding underlines the importance of matching the instruction to the specific cognitive weakness of the child. The Naglieri and Gottling study was the first to examine the efficacy of facilitation of planning as part of mathematics instruction for learning-disabled students.

The Naglieri–Gottling (1997) Study

The investigators worked with a sample of elementary school students who attended an independent school that specialized in the treatment of students with significant learning problems and who had made minimal progress in public special education programs. The two teachers who provided instruction to the students at the school participated in the study and were consulted every week by the authors about the application of the intervention, the monitoring of the students' progress, and the facilitation of classroom discus-sions. Over a two-month period, the students participated in seven baseline and 21 intervention sessions.

The intervention sessions consisted of three 10-minute periods— one for completing a math page, one for facilitating planning, and one for mathematics again. During the group discussion periods, self-reflection and evaluation, verbalization of methods used, and discussion were encouraged with the goal of improving planning competence. One student's comment often became the starting point for vigorous discussion and further development of the idea he/she had raised. Some of the prompts used by the teachers to encourage discussion are listed here. These are quoted to show how planning processes emerge from collaborative learning and how "zones of proximal development" are expanded; both lead to a better performance in subsequent arithmetic tasks.

- Can anyone tell me anything about these problems?
- Let's talk about how you did the worksheet.
- Why did you do it that way?
- How did you solve the problems?

- What could you have done to get more correct answers?
- What did it teach you?
- What else did you notice about how this page was done?
- What will you do next time?
- What did you think of that?
- I noticed that many of you did not do what you said was important.

In response to these probes, the students made comments such as the following:

- I'll do all the easy ones first.
- I do them row by row.
- When I get distracted, I'll move my seat.
- I have to remember to borrow.
- I do the ones with ones, zeros and tens in them—they're easy.
- If it is a big problem (all big numbers on the top), you don't have to borrow, so do it first.
- Be sure to get them right, not just get them done.
- I have to stay awake.
- I have to remember to add the numbers after multiplying.
- I have to keep the columns straight.

Note that the teachers made no direct statements, such as "That is correct" or "Remember to use that same strategy." Nor did they give instruction in mathematics or provide any feedback about the number of correct answers obtained. Their role was to facilitate self-reflection, and thereby to encourage the students to plan, so that they could complete the worksheets successfully.

As mentioned earlier, the results of the intervention showed that the low and high groups benefited differentially from the intervention, despite the fact that the two groups had similar initial baseline scores in math computation. Students who were low in planning improved consistently across the intervention segments, whereas the students with initial high planning scores improved somewhat, but inconsistently.

Planning is at the Center of Remediation

We use many tools for teaching and learning; our most important tool, however, is language. Language not only shapes our thoughts and guides our learning but also enables us to communicate our thoughts to others.

While an animal may remember something by repeated direct experience, humans can use language to remember a vast number of things and ideas. Planning is, similarly, greatly helped by the use of language. This does not necessarily have to take the form of external speech; it may be internalized private speech. How does this work? In remediation, the adult's directions are often repeated aloud by the child; this is an example of external speech. However, once the child has internalized the directions, he/she may not need to repeat the directions any more, not even silently in his/her mind; the external speech is transformed to an inner voice which now regulates the child's behavior. We see this often in PREP sessions. The facilitator asks the child, "How did you do this?", and the child responds, "I just did it! Don't ask me how!" This child cannot translate his or her inner speech to external speech, yet the inner speech is guiding and regulating his/her behavior.

Essentials of Planning

What exactly do we try to boost when we set out to help children develop their planning skills? The following very brief discussion outlines the bare essentials (see Das, Kar, and Parrila, 1996 for a full discussion of this issue).

At the center of planning are goals and objectives. Before a problem can be solved or a composition written, we need to establish what our goals are; then we can plan. In the Naglieri and Gottling study (1997), the teacher asked, "Can anyone tell me anything about these problems?" In other words, the children were being asked to define their goals and objectives. Our goals may change as we progress through a task; we may set ourselves immediate, intermediate, and final goals, and make appropriate plans to fulfil the goals at each stage.

Planning has four components—anticipation, representation, execution, and regulation, not necessarily in that order. We anticipate when we try to imagine what will happen if we do one thing rather than another, often using our past experiences in similar situations as a guide; if we can anticipate what is going to happen, we are prepared for it. Representation of the problem is equally important. Essentially, representation involves answering the question, "What is this task all about?" Execution is about carrying out the task step by step, and regulation involves paying attention to the outcomes as we perform the task, and if necessary adjusting our activities as a consequence—in other words, monitoring our activities according to the goals and objectives that we established.

The Application of Planning in the Writing of Compositions

The Naglieri and Gottling study (1997) showed that PREP tasks can be oriented to focus on planning and attention in the remediation of arithmetic disability. Another academic task in which planning is of vital importance is the writing of compositions. Of course, children need to have mastered the elements of grammar in order to write, just as they need to have learned the simple mechanics of adding, subtracting, multiplying, and dividing before they can do arithmetical calculations. Once they have those basic skills, however, planning is the most important component in writing essays and doing sums. Can we help children improve their composition writing skills by improving their planning and organizational skills? Though this area has not yet been specifically addressed by PREP, it should be possible to construct global and bridging tasks that focus on planning with particular reference to writing. Let us look, for example, at a passage from Tolstoy's novel *The Death of Ivan Ilych* (1967):

It was morning. He knew it was morning because Gerasim had gone, and Peter the footman had come and put out the candles, drawn back one of the curtains, and begun quietly to tidy up. Whether it was morning or evening, Friday or Sunday, made no difference, it was all just the same: the gnawing, unmitigated, agonizing pain never ceasing for an instant, the consciousness of life inexorably waning but not yet extinguished, the approach of that ever dreaded and hateful Death which was the only reality, and always the same falsity. What were days, weeks, hours, in such a case?

Does this passage have a goal and an objective? Obviously, yes; it describes the feelings of a dying man. Does it succeed in its representation of the theme? Again, yes; the man's pain and suffering are clearly and superbly expressed. Does it build up anticipation? Very definitely, yes; it is clear from the first two sentences what is going to happen in the rest of the paragraph—the despair, the indifference, the transcendental view of reality. Is it executed adequately? There is no doubt that it is. Does the author regulate (that is, control) the flow of the narrative? Yes, definitely, one can see the chain of control from the simple statement that sets the stage ("It was morning") to the philosophical musing with which the passage ends. Thus this is an excellent example of a planned composition, in which the author utilized the four components of planning to create the effect that he desired.

Here is another passage, from Salman Rushdie's *Haroun and the Sea of Stories* (1991), which could easily be understood by a 12-year-old child:

> After his mother left home, Haroun found that he couldn't keep his mind on anything for very long or, to be precise, for more than eleven minutes at a time. Rashid took him to a movie to cheer him up, but after exactly eleven minutes Haroun's attention wandered, and when the film ended, he had no idea how it all turned out, and had to ask Rashid if the good guys won in the end. The next day Haroun was playing goalie in a neighborhood game of street hockey, and after pulling off a string of brilliant saves in the first eleven minutes, he began to let in the softest, most foolish and most humiliating of goals. And so it went on: his mind was always wandering off somewhere and leaving his body behind.

Passages such as this one by Rushdie could be used in a remedial program to give children an idea of the essentials of planning that are operative in good compositions.

Five Features for Judging a Composition

Generally speaking, compositions can be rated on a scale of poor to excellent—a well-planned composition has some specific characteristics as discussed by Das et al. (1996). These are the features on which a composition can be rated good, medium, or poor—*expression, organization, wording, mechanics,* and *individuality.*

1. *Expression:* It appears that thought has been given to this story, or the essay. The writer says what is meant, points relate to the topic, and there is no padding. In contrast, in a poor expression, it is hard to tell what the writer is saying, it makes little sense, and it gives the impression of trying to get something on paper.
2. *Organization:* The organized composition has a good starting point, has a sense of direction of movement in the story, appears to have an underlying plan, and seems logically arranged. A poorly organized composition starts anywhere and never gets somewhere; ideas are presented randomly with no apparent forethought.
3. *Wording:* Good wording figures uncommon words, or words in unusual combinations, which shows imagination. Poor wording employs words carelessly, there are many mistakes in usage, and the wording is not clear.
4. *Mechanics:* A good composition has no serious errors in sentence structure. Punctuation is correct, and spelling is consistent and appropriate for the child's grade in school. In the case of poor mechanics, there are serious errors in sentence structure, making the story difficult to understand; many punctuation errors make the story fragmented.
5. *Individuality:* There is a unique or creative approach to the material, unusual or original ideas give story a twist. Poor individuality is characterized by no originality; the ideas are mundane, not creative, and uninteresting.

Let us examine the Haroun story on each of these rating criteria. The most important features here seem to be expression, organization, and individuality. The wording and mechanics have no outstanding characteristics, except that they are adequate. So, we ask in judging the story, has thought been given to the story and does the writer say what is meant? Obviously, the expression is clear and it catches our attention right away.

Next is organization. Does it have a good starting point and a direction? Is the underlying plan apparent and logical? Yes, again. Haroun found that he could not keep his mind on anything very long and this passage ends with his mind always wandering off somewhere and leaving his body behind.

Does the narrative show individuality? Yes, it is unique and creative in its approach to a simple fact—a boy whose mind wanders. This in itself is a commonplace topic, but the writer makes it an outstanding narrative. Obviously, it is a piece of creative writing that delights the reader and will make an impression as being unusual and unique.

To sum up, the point of the discussion on uses of planning is that we have a cognitive theory of planning that can be applied for facilitating problem solving and composition. Without a theoretical basis, it will be impossible to know where to begin, to help children who have difficulties in these areas. I hope the preceding discussion will guide the construction of global and bridging tasks that focus on planning, in particular reference to mathematical problem solving and writing composition. These are two areas that have not been specifically addressed in PREP.

16

Integration of Contemporary Views on Reading

The interpretation of reading difficulties can be wrapped up by presenting examples of studies that integrate Luria's notion, as we discussed earlier in Chapter 7, with contemporary views. This chapter is a scientific report, written in the style of an article in an academic journal. So, I hope that psychologists and other academics will find it worth reading. Is it of interest to teachers? For every one of them! Why not?

The inability to engage in phonological coding has been suggested as the major cause of reading disability for children (Stanovich, 1988; Torgesen et al., 1994). Researchers generally agree that phonological processing plays an important role in early reading. One of the most frequently cited articles in the field (Torgesen et al., 1994) argues that phonological processing abilities are causally related to normal acquisition of reading skills. Support for this claim can also be found in the relationship between pre-readers' phonological processing scores and their reading development after one to three years (for example, Bradley and Bryant, 1985). A review by Share and Stanovich (1995) concluded that there is virtually unassailable evidence that poor readers, as a group, are impaired in a very wide range of basic cognitive tasks in the phonological domain (1995: 9).

The belief that phonological coding is a "bottleneck" process deficit in dyslexia has been reiterated by Frith (1999). She reflects the emerging consensus that dyslexia is a condition marked by a phonological deficit. She suggests that dyslexia should be defined in conjunction with three levels of manifestation—biological, cognitive, and behavioral. Each of these levels interacts with the cultural environment. According to her, dyslexia is a neurodevelopmental disorder with a biological origin. Brain activation studies, in which Frith is a coauthor, have recently shown that dyslexics have significantly lower levels of activation, localized in parts of the temporal–occipital region (Paulesu et al., 2001).

A distinction has been made between the true dyslexic, with specific cognitive difficulties, and the so-called garden-variety poor reader (Stanovich, 1988). The general poor reader should not be included within the broad category of dyslexics, as poor performance in reading does not necessarily imply a neurodevelopmental disorder. Poor reading can result from a variety of reasons, such as poor instruction, lack of motivation, health and emotional problems, and/or lack of cultural literacy, as well as environmental disadvantages, such as inadequate and low general intelligence. Some of these deficiencies can be removed through tutoring and remedial reading programs. With regard to a strict application of the category dyslexia, there is an apparent heterogeneity. Surface and deep dyslexia, delayed speed in word reading, are different from the inaccurate reading of words and pseudo-words (phonological dyslexia), and have been discussed in the literature. A recent theoretical review, proposing how one transforms the printed word to speech (Coltheart et al., 2001), discusses some of these different kinds of dyslexia and attempts to integrate them by using the familiar concepts in reading—orthographic analysis, grapheme–phoneme correspondence, semantic coding, and phonological output lexicon.

But the question is—can we assume that both word-reading difficulty and phonological coding deficits among children can be related to fundamental problems in cognitive processing, as measured by tasks that do not require reading? Or, is reading perhaps a module separate from general cognitive processing? The literature on reading is vast and varied, and, therefore, we will answer these concerns within the context of PASS theory.

Children with specific reading difficulties in decoding written words (in English) are distinguished from generally poor readers. Specific deficiencies are detected by a limited number of tests. These include immediate sequential recall of word or digit series (order rather than item memory), rapid naming of letters, simple familiar words, familiar colors and objects, speed repetition of words and pseudo-words (speech rate), and also phonological awareness tests

(Kirby, Booth and Das, 1996). Frith (1985) depicts these as the watershed measures that characterize individuals with specific reading disabilities or dyslexia.

Does the source of dyslexia lie in cognitive skills that are found only in reading-related tasks, in tasks related to phonology, or in a more fundamental process identifiable in nonreading tasks as well (Das, 1995a)? The latter are sometimes referred to as distal processes, in contrast to the former, which are referred to as proximal processes. Torgesen et al. (1987) identified three subprocesses of the proximal kind—knowledge of letters and letter combinations, a spoken lexicon that is necessary for recognizing the words after they are spoken, and phonetic recoding in working memory that is helpful in maintaining the spoken word in working memory. Coltheart et al. (2001) explain the visual recognition of words and pseudo-words, but do not concern themselves with speech inputs and the phonological recoding of speech. How does a spoken word get analyzed and produce a speech response, as when we are asked to repeat a word we have just heard? Dyslexics and poor readers are sometimes unable to repeat an unfamiliar or a pseudo-word, perhaps because that too involves a phonological conversion (Patterson and Shewell's model cited in Coltheart et al., 2001).

Phonological processing, then, appears to be required in both speech repetition and in reading aloud from print. Poor reading and its restricted variation, dyslexia, are characterized, essentially, by a deficit in phonological recoding. It is reasonable to regard both as speech-related deficits. "The processing of speech sounds has been targeted as the critical link between spoken and written languages," writes Frith (1999: 202), supporting the early research of Bradley and Bryant (1985). She continues, "There is robust evidence that difficulties in the acquisition of reading are related to difficulties in the ability to segment the stream of speech" (ibid.).

In view of the preceding discussion, there are strong grounds for believing that the distal processes that influence reading and speech repetition must have a common requirement for phonological recoding. In our view, the distal processes may include working memory and knowledge base, but, additionally, one or all of the four

PASS processes. These contribute to the acquisition of phonological and orthographic skills (important for spelling) as well as to strategies for appropriate application (Das, 1995a; Das, Parrila and Papadopoulos, 2000).

An Illustrative Study on the Role of Successive Processing

Within the context of distal and proximal variables, we present a study that explores the cognitive profiles of reading-disabled children and nonimpaired readers. PASS tests that were earlier forms of the Das-Naglieri Cognitive Assessment System (CAS) (1987) were used (Kirby et al., 1996). A reading test for word decoding (word identification and pseudo-word reading) and passage comprehension was administered to all three groups, along with the tests for Planning, Attention, Simultaneous, and Successive processing. These tests are described in the following paragraphs, so that it will be possible to discuss the nature of dyslexia revealed by tests of PASS processes.

The two Planning tests that were used are Planned Connections and Visual Search. The Planned Connections subtest involves connecting adjacent numbers and combinations of numbers to numbers, and numbers to letters, that is, 1 to 2, and 2 to 3, and likewise with letters, 1 to A, A to 2, and 2 to B. In contrast, the Visual Search subtest includes tasks such as searching for a target picture among other pictures, searching for a target number among numbers, and for a target letter among letters.

The Attention test consists of the Expressive Attention and Receptive Attention subtests. The Expressive Attention subtest is similar to the Stroop test. (In this test, for example, the word 'BLUE' is printed in yellow color, and word 'YELLOW' is printed in blue color. You are asked to name the color of the print, not the word, which is the source of confusion.) The Receptive Attention subtest involves identifying letter pairs that are visually identical, such as aa, dd, and in the more difficult form of the task, the identification of the same letters in uppercase and lowercase combinations, such as aA, Dd. The latter form of the task requires lexical access.

The Simultaneous Processing tests were the familiar Matrix Analogies, similar to Raven's Progressive Matrices and Figure Memory, which in turn is similar to Memory for Designs (Das et al., 1979).

Successive Processing tests were comprised of Word Series, involving short-term memory for short lists of one-syllable words, Sentence Repetition, Naming Time, and Speech Rate. These four tests, along with Color–Word Reading in the Expressive Attention subtest, have been designated as the watershed tests in discriminating between dyslexics and nondyslexics, as mentioned earlier.

Results confirmed the hypothesis that the group of children with average IQs, but with a designated reading disability, had poorer scores mainly in Successive Processing tasks. The comparison group comprised children of the same age.

The other hypothesis concerned reading and age. It was expected that the children with average IQs (in Grades 4 and 5) and a reading disability would not differ in their performance on Successive tests when compared to younger children of an equivalent reading level (for example, in Grade 2). This was confirmed. This result is interesting for the subtyping of dyslexics discussed ahead. The reading-disabled group resembled the delayed dyslexic group, which may not have a damaged phonological system according to Harm and Seidenberg (1999) and Pugh et al. (2000). Table 16.1 presents the results of the study.

Table 16.1 Results of t Tests for PASS and Reading Variables for Three Planned Contrasts

	Contrast			
	ARD vs CAC		ARD vs RAC	
Measure	t	p	t	p
Planning				
Planned Connections	2.492	.019	2.492	.019
Visual Search	.668	ns	2.651	.013
Attention				
Expressive	.665	ns	1.865	.073
Receptive	2.681	.012	.239	ns
Simultaneous				
Matrix Analogies	5.116	<.00!	1.834	.077
Figure Memory	.933	ns	1.743	.092

Table 16.1 continued

Table 16.1 continued

| Measure | Contrast | | | |
| | ARD vs CAC | | ARD vs RAC | |
	t	p	t	p
Successive				
Word Series	2.588	0.15	1.599	ns
Sentence Repetition	1.922	0.65	.504	ns
Naming Time	4.840	<.001	.987	ns
Speech Rate	1.824	.079	.798	ns
Reading				
Word Attack	6.207	<.001	.949	ns
Word Identification	6.159	<.001	.458	ns
Passage Comprehension	6.039	<.001	.154	ns
Grade Equivalent	8.684	<.001	.379	ns

Note: Probabilities of .10 or greater are shown as ns. All the tests are two-tailed and df = 28. Comparing Average IQ Reading-Disabled (ARD), Grade 4/5 Chronological Age Controls (CAC), and Grade 2 Reading Age Controls (RAC). This is from an unpublished study by J.P. Das and T. Papadopoulos from the Developmental Disability center at the University of Alberta.

We can explain some of the differences in other tests that do not belong to the class of Successive tests. For example, both Planned Connections and Receptive Attention require encoding of letters and lexical access. In conclusion, Kirby, Booth, and Das stated, "These results point to the critical role of successive processing in reading achievement and to the need for remediation to address successive processing" (1996: 442).

A Study on Naming Time and Speech Rate

The illustrative studies strongly suggest that successive processing can unite the various core correlates of word decoding; its binding strength increases if the word is a pseudo-word and increases further if it is to be read aloud, requiring pronunciation. The correlates are speech rate (fast repetition of three simple words), naming time (for naming simple, short, and familiar words arranged in rows, naming rows of single letters, or digits and color strips), and short-term memory for short lists of simple and short words. Of these tasks, speech rate correlates best with decoding pseudo-words. While the correlation with naming time is the next best one, it has a slight edge over speech rate in decoding short familiar words. These results need to be replicated although they are consistent with the theory that poor reading is a speech-related process.

A stepwise multiple regression analysis, predicting word identification (real words), revealed that naming time contributed most, followed by speech rate, phonemic segmentation, and serial recall (of one-syllable word strings). The prediction of Word Attack (pseudo-word reading) score showed an advantage for speech rate over naming time. Speech rate emerged as a strong predictor, followed by phonemic segmentation, naming time, and serial word recall.

It is reasonable to accept that word attack or pseudo-word decoding skill will be more closely related to phonemic segmentation than word identification. But in both kinds of word decoding, speech rate was better than phonemic segmentation. Do we not infer from these results that, apparently, a distal factor such as speech rate is a better predictor than a proximal one?

A Study on Prediction of Reading Difficulties

Another ongoing longitudinal study exemplifies the usefulness of the distal PASS processes in predicting reading difficulty (Papadopoulus, Parrila, and Kirby, 1998). PASS processing tasks, together with several phonological coding tasks, were administered to 90 kindergarten children identified by their teachers as being at risk for early reading problems. Two reading tasks (word attack and word identification) were administered a year later in Grade 1, when children were exposed to reading instruction. Results showed that performance on both successive processing and phonological tasks at the kindergarten class correlated significantly with reading skills one year later. We note that the group of high-risk children did not include exclusively dyslexic children, rather it was a mixed group designated by their teachers. Some of the high-risk children turned out to have normal reading scores (that is, 30th percentile or above) in reading real and pseudo-words. Three types of tests, phonological, successive, and simultaneous, together distinguished between those children who were diagnosed as reading-disabled and the normal readers in Grade 1. The risk of remaining a nonreader, in turn, was predicted by an extremely poor level of functioning on two successive and two phonological tasks.

We conclude, then, that the true dyslexic is characterized by a specific deficit in successive processing, in spite of an average or above average score on the three remaining processes, whereas the generally poor reader may have lower than average scores on some of the three other PASS measures as well. There are two other possible PASS profiles:

1. Some poor readers may not have a subaverage score in any of the PASS tests; the explanation for poor reading could be found variously in the absence of a literacy environment, poor instruction, and/or detrimental motivational and emotional conditions.

2. Even among dyslexics, there can be heterogeneous groups in terms of their performance in successive tests. This latter possibility was raised first by Torgesen and Houck (1980) and discussed further by Torgesen (1982). These investigators had identified a group of poor readers who performed at the average level in short-term memory (STM) measures (digit span, letter span, and word span). The issue has resurfaced in the discussion of double deficit. Double deficit is a deficit in phonological awareness as distinguished from a deficit in rapid automatic naming, of not only letters and words, but also colors and objects (Wolf and Bowers, 1999). The suggestion, open to argument, is that some dyslexics may have one or the other deficit, with those having both being the poorest readers.

Can Luria's conceptualization of successive processing and CAS measures of successive processing help in understanding the issue? Luria viewed successive processing in terms of a sequence of movements as much as organizing ideas and events in succession (Luria, 1966a: 74, 1973; Das et al., 1979). Both execution of a series of movements smoothly, such as continuing a series of writing (for example, +++--+++--+++--) and fast articulation of a fixed series of words (for example, cat–wall–hot, cat–wall–hot), which Luria termed kinetic melody, make a minimal demand on memory. However, the first task has almost no load on STM, as the series is visually accessible at any time during the performance.

Speech rate, we suggest, is closer to a kinetic melody. Inasmuch as the rehearsal part of the phonological loop is close to the kinetic melody description, it represents successive processing. It also shares the same general region of the brain as associated with successive processing. Our research has made use of both kinds of successive tasks (Das, Naglieri, and Kirby, 1994). Among the subtests of CAS, we include speech rate (cat–wall–hot, cat–wall–hot), serial recall of words, sentence repetition (Naglieri and Das, 1997: 145), and naming speed for simple high frequency words (not included in the CAS). These tests have been used in predicting reading ability. A fresh look at successive processing is warranted in the light of new findings on the brain-related correlates of the reading process. We have held on to the view that successive processing is not solely verbal and simultaneous processing is not solely nonverbal (Das et al., 1979), following Luria. The nonverbal part of successive processing is illustrated by the task called series completion (+++--...) and by similar tasks, such as copying hand movements and reconstructing a serial order of turning a row of five to seven chips presented in a predetermined random order, as previously used (Das, Naglieri and Kirby, 1994). Perhaps, successive processing can be divided into two kinds of operations—verbal operations, which require phonological coding, and nonverbal operations, which require reconstructing the temporal order of movements. Both share the overarching process of serial ordering. Such a division may be related to deficiencies in two anatomical components—the magnocellular system and the cerebellar functions. Both of these deficiencies can cause difficulties in recoding and in the production of movements in a temporal order. As briefly reviewed by Frith (1999: 206):

> If expressed at the cognitive level, both theories may imply a temporal processing deficit. Fast temporal processing may be a basic characteristic of all perceptual systems, visual as well as auditory, object-based as well as speech-based. Slower-than-normal perceptual processing might well compromise the development of a phonological system.

The results of our most recent investigation into this issue suggest that phonological awareness alone is an insufficient predictor of reading development. We will refer to a longitudinal study of children from kindergarten to Grade 3. In this study it was shown that verbal STM measures such as serial word recall as well as naming speed remained as viable predictors, even when letter recognition ability and phonological awareness were partialled out (Parrila and Kirby, 2000). These results could not be obtained if a phonological deficit alone was sufficient.

In our concluding comments we do not have to ask the rhetorical question—Is Luria relevant? Instead, we suggest looking beyond the narrow confines of phonological awareness in order to gain a better understanding of reading and its connection to language.

A Look beyond Phonological Coding

In a strict modular view as depicted by Fodor (1983), language is an independent ability that is practically insular to cognitive development. It is an innate ability, waiting to be triggered by environmental experience. This position is being questioned. For example, Kuhl (2000) argues from a neuroscience perspective that the newborn brain is not yet lateralized for language, raising doubts for a strong module viewpoint. Karmiloff-Smith (1992) does not support a strict modular position with regard to language, describing its development as "modularization". From these recent and contemporary perspectives, it is easier to view reading as connected to a semantic or a conceptual system, related to—rather than strictly isolated from—cognitive processing in general, a view that will be still consistent with a weak modular hypothesis.

In the final section of this chapter, we discuss some contemporary issues in reading and examine the usefulness of Luria's notions and the PASS theory.

Naming Objects and Reading Words: A Theoretical Connection

We return to Rapid Automatic Naming (RAN) as an example. Here we ask—why should the naming of objects be significantly predictable for naming words, unless the two share some fundamental cognitive processes, as discussed earlier while reviewing successive processing?

A recent study by Bowers, Vigliocco, Stadthagen-Gonzalez, and Vinson (1999) caught our attention. This study offered both theoretical reasoning and experimental evidence, demonstrating that the perception of objects and written words share some common features. These common features include grammatical encoding, phonological (syntactic) encoding, and articulation demand. They differ in that object recognition involves a semantic or conceptual system, whereas for naming written words, a syntactic system is sufficient. The syntactic system interacts with the semantic one; without such an interrelation, the reader would not automatically search for a meaning, when presented with a pseudo-word, let alone a real word. However, the search may not always be successful. Further, the presence of syntactic and semantic interaction explains why a word in the text of a sentence and paragraph may be read faster than when presented in isolation (Pollasteck and Rayner, 1993).

In Figure 16.1, we have attempted to present the relationship between selected components of object naming and reading. Part of the figure also shows the relationship with the two PASS processes, simultaneous and successive processing. External information to be processed is shown in the three dark gray boxes—Naming Objects, Oral Reading, and Articulation Object (also color patches) naming starts with a perceptual system; so does a written word. Articulation is an external event that has a speech output; it works as external information for processing speech when the individual is required to read aloud. The palest shading represents internal events—these are semantic, object's name, visual, phonological, assembled, as well as two consequences of articulation. The only one of the internal events that clearly acts as a piece of information to be processed is the object name. Since finding the name and processing it further are both internal events, their shading is very pale. All of these remarks are speculative but we hope they will be generally accepted.

The other labels relate predominantly, but by no means solely, to simultaneous and successive processing operations that characterize the mental events. The two other PASS components, Planning and Attention, are involved in various degrees, along with the two

Figure 16.1   The Relationship between Object-Naming and Reading

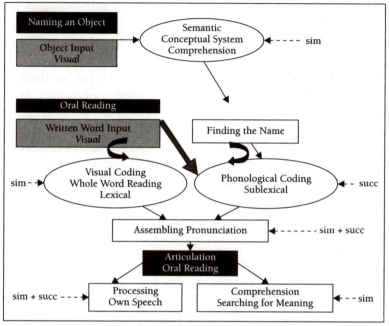

Source: Author.

preeminent processes. Objects can be named by linking the perception of the object to a conceptual system (Bowers et al., 1999); inasmuch as it involves categorization and labeling, the semantic/conceptual system is utilizing a knowledge base. But finding the name of the observed object is a matching process, which is a simultaneous operation. Object naming from this point onward shares the same processing and output components, except that the reader is denied direct visual access to the object's name. Therefore, it is suggested that unlike whole-word reading, naming the object (or a color patch or ideograph) is a phonologically recoded procedure that produces a sublexically accessed name. However, one may argue otherwise and propose that the word for the object appear as an image, and then it may be read as a whole.

Phonological recoding involves mainly successive processing as we have argued earlier, both on the basis of the theory and its correlation with tests of successive processing. Assembling pronunciation requires a sequencing activity as well as matching with an item in the lexicon for pronunciation (knowledge base). Processing one's own speech, we suggest, involves both simultaneous and successive processes.

Finally, articulation is a sequential speech act, but we think it may require motor planning, unless articulation is automated. Articulation of pseudo-words and long or unfamiliar words requires both successive processing and deliberate (not automatic) planning. With regard to comprehension, we have suggested that this is the same as a conceptual system, predominantly requiring simultaneous processing and a knowledge base.

Reading and STM

Three other issues alluded to earlier, will be discussed briefly. The first one is the double deficit (Wolf and Bowers, 1999). This implies dissociation between STM-related aspects of word-decoding deficit and RAN. The second is the characterization of the phonological loop. The third relates to heterogeneous groups of dyslexics. All three are connected in various ways and have implications for the PASS model as well. This part of the book recognizes the contemporary issues, but awaits further research.

The double or dual deficits are found among a majority of dyslexics, as Wolf and Bowers (1999) have suggested. Only a minority of dyslexics exclusively show either a RAN or STM deficit. How do we understand it in the context of a successive processing deficit that, according to our research, is preeminently prevalent among the true dyslexics, that is, those with a specific rather than pervasive cognitive deficit? The PASS theory and tests have included both types of measures. STM and Working Memory are required in processing serial recall (Word Series, Sentence Repetition, and Sentence Question in the CAS), whereas Speech Rate, Naming Time and Color Naming (see Das, Naglieri, and Kirby, 1994 for a review of PASS tests) share the essential operations of RAN. According to the double deficit hypothesis, should these two sets of tasks load on separate orthogonal factors? We cannot find any evidence either in favor of or against it. On the other hand, the factors may be substantially correlated as both share the same successive processing.

Phonological Loop Components

A discussion of new notions on the phonological loop, which was first proposed as an articulatory loop and later reformulated, follows (Gathercole and Baddley, 1989). New elaborations are offered by Burgess and Hitch (1999). In their extensive and comprehensive review, two relevant concepts are the two components of the loop—rehearsal and phonological store. Recent brain imaging research, as well as traditional brain lesion data, supports this division.

Rehearsal activity is associated with Broca's area, whereas the phonological store is either in Wernicke's area or in an area slightly behind it. The review by Burgess and Hitch (1999) confirms what has been known for some time—that phonological coding and rehearsal have separate cortical locations. Its implication for the present discussion, however, is important. Consult Figure 16.1, which is an elaboration mostly of phonological store, rather than rehearsal. Reading is related to STM and rehearsal via the phonological store. Simply, we can suggest that STM, as captured in memory span, is a function of the number of items that can be rehearsed in a unit of time (articulation), and that itself must depend on the length of the word, on the one hand, and the speed of phonological encoding of the word, which must precede articulation, on the other. Remembering a short list of familiar words is distinguished from repetition of an infrequently occurring long word; these two operations are connected with rehearsal and phonological store (Burgess and Hitch, 1999). Listening to one's own speech is a necessary step in accommodating rapid automatized naming of objects, as well as in reading aloud. We can suggest that RAN essentially requires a successive processing activity, in addition to being modulated by phonological encoding as shown in various parts of Figure 16.1. Thus, RAN is both a separate and a correlated operation, combining mechanisms that end in articulation and rehearsal.

Two kinds of dyslexia are suggested by Harm and Seidenberg (1999), namely, phonological and delayed dyslexia. Both can be related to phonological store and rehearsal mechanisms as well. Phonological dyslexia is the typical and more frequent kind of dyslexia. It is theoretically explained as a damage or deficit to the phonological store; such weakness impedes rehearsal due to poor phonological representation of a word that is required to be read and recalled. In the case of the delayed dyslexia, the dyslexic may have an underdeveloped knowledge base for exceptional or irregular words (for example, touch, though, isle, knead). The orthography and pronunciation of such words require more rote learning than phonological coding of grapheme to phoneme. The exact reason for the delayed development of the phonological knowledge store is, however, unclear. What happens, to be reasonable, is that the exceptional words are to be processed as whole words, and require lexical rather than sublexical processing.

Kinds of Dyslexia: Can PASS Theory and Luria Help?

Considering the distinction proposed by Harm and Seidenberg (1999), we suppose that the phonological dyslexics, the most prevalent group among dyslexics, are likely to have a deficit in successive processing, whereas the delayed dyslexics are likely to have a mixed deficit in some of the other processes as well. This explanation may be only a partial one; its object is to show the relevance of PASS processes.

An issue that requires further research is delineating the nature of garden-variety dyslexia. The true garden-variety dyslexics who are poor readers in spite of adequate instruction, environmental conditions, and normal emotional characteristics may have a variety of processing deficits, rather than a specific deficit as our previous research indicated (Das, Mensink, and Mishra, 1990).

Both kinds of dyslexics are poor in decoding pseudo-words, although they might have partially overcome their inability to read real words. A recent study (Pugh et al., 2000) of adult dyslexics without neurological impairment shows connections within the brain areas activated during reading to be different between dyslexics and nondyslexics; the implication of its results are significant to Luria's relevance. Consider the following neuro-psychological aspects.

The pathways in the brain that are initiated by seeing a word have been known for some years (Patton, Sundsten, Crill, and Swanson, 1976). Visual reception activates the lateral geniculate nucleus in the thalamus, and travels to the primary visual area, and then on to a higher order visual area. It connects to the angular gyrus, which is the tertiary association area of the parietal–occipital–temporal region, one of the overlapping zones (Luria, 1973). According to Patton et al. (1976), the sequence continues, activating Wernicke's area, then Broca's, and, finally, the facial area of the motor cortex, which results in the articulation of the word. A recent article by Pugh et al. (2000) identifies the tertiary area, mainly in the angular gyrus, to be the hub of word processing. However, their report does not examine the sequence of activity as the old research of Patton et al. (1976) did. Nevertheless, it concludes from functional Magnetic Resonance Imaging (fMRI) that the activation at the site of the angular gyrus had strong connections with the visual association area and Wernicke's area, during the tasks that required phonological coding. The tasks involved distinguishing between uppercase and lowercase consonant strings, and between two consonants that rhyme (example of tasks that have low demand on phonological coding). Two other high phonologically demanding tasks were also given to the dyslexic adults. These required the individuals to distinguish between two pseudo-words that do or do not rhyme, and between two real words that may or may not have the same meaning. The dyslexic adults did not show activation of the angular gyrus while doing the latter two tasks (Pugh et al., 2000). One obvious comment is that those persons with dyslexia were unable to carry out phonological coding. If this is the case, the results confirm that the brain images correspond to what is known behaviorally.

An important conclusion from this new research is that among people with dyslexia, intact activation pathways are preserved and used when phonological processing is within the individual's ability. There is no sign of a global destruction of these functional connections. The connections can develop if appropriate remediation or intervention programs are instituted early during the developmental period. Remedial methods to enhance reading had focused on enhancing the two PASS processes, namely, successive and simultaneous processing. This is the PREP program that has been effective in strengthening word decoding (Das, 1999; Das, Naglieri, and Kirby, 1994). However, proper experiments using an "aptitude by treatment interaction" for specific kinds of dyslexics (for example, true dyslexics vs garden variety, phonological vs naming speed deficit, delayed/surface vs phonological dyslexic, successive vs non-successive) are yet to be carried out. Then, we may have clearer guidance for specific remediation for dyslexia.

The Relevance of Luria

We can say, after this brief review on the applications of Luria's notions of the functional division of the brain and their elaboration in PASS theory and CAS, that Luria is still relevant. Dyslexia as a separate and distinct syndrome can be limited to difficulties mainly in successive processing among beginning readers, and in the planning and allocation of attentional resources as children learn strategies for using orthography in writing and composition. A plea for diagnosing dyslexia beyond word recognition and pseudo-word reading accuracy and speed is inherent in recent literature as we move into studying adult dyslexics, some of whom are fully compensated and have mastered word reading. If we are looking for cognitive markers, the PASS theory, we may say, has been helpful and should be elaborated. Even in delineating brain locations for dyslexia, Luria's broad functional organizations are relevant; the more active areas among normal readers were in the temporal area, and the area of overlap between occipital and temporal regions. The frontotemporal region was found to be involved in making decisions between pseudo-words and real words amongst readers of English, whereas with Italians reading Italian (more transparent orthography), the brain activation was in the left superior temporal regions (Paulesu et al., 2001). Perhaps the English readers are not sure how to read a pseudo-word until they can decide that it is not one of the irregular words, of which there are many in the language. The Lurian approach also guides remediation by first determining whether an individual child with poor reading has the telltale deficit in his/her PASS cognitive profile. If there is no significant disparity between the four PASS processes, the cause of poor reading performance may lie in cultural conditions, or personality and motivational aspects. In a recent clinical case, an 8-year-old girl showed poor reading and very poor numerical knowledge, and yet had average scores across the four PASS processes. Lack of motivation to continue with tasks when they increased in difficulty, poor instruction, and unconditionally rewarding grandparents, who were bringing up the girl, were discovered as the main explanations for her poor performance. Improvement in motivation as well as strengthening her reading can be attempted through manipulating PREP tasks. In contrast, another clinical case of a poor reader who was significantly poor in planning but with a high performance on simultaneous and low successive processing would receive a kind of remedial program which trained the child in planning and successive processes. PREP can be manipulated to focus on one or the other process (Das, 1999). Thus, the neo-Lurian approach enables us to measure and diagnose strengths and weaknesses in cognitive processes that characterize poor readers and dyslexics; it also prescribes remediation. Much remains to be done in exploring unexplained reading disability; with regard to PASS, new discoveries in brain activities will compel us to expand and revise Luria's notions, especially about planning and successive processes.

Epilogue: New Horizons in Understanding Reading

In the previous chapter we reviewed some selected research that is expanding our understanding of *reading and the rate at which a reader reads*. We were able to provide a framework from PASS theory and neuropsychology. In this epilogue, we continue the review of contemporary concerns in reading and failure to read by focusing on two basic components of reading.

Phonological Awareness and Rapid Automatic Naming: Two Cores of the Same Fruit

It has been known for some years now that both phonological awareness and rapid automatic naming (RAN) speed are associated with reading. But what do these tongue twisters mean? Both describe the new reader's ability to use and understand rhymes, and detect and manipulate sounds. My preliterate 4-year-old son surprised us one day when he overheard me helping my 7-year-old sister spell the word *cobbler*. He jumped in with "It's *cobb* then *ler*", demonstrating that he had already acquired the basic principle of segmenting words into sounds. The two children enjoyed playing the "secret codes" word game: "When I say jara, you know I am saying raja (king), when I say nira I mean rani (queen)." We also played with spoonerisms, such as *learty hunch* means hearty lunch, *gaterwate* means watergate, and *tice noy* means nice toy. By the age of five, he enjoyed playing the *take the sound away* game: "If I was carrying a chair, and a strong wind blew the *ch* away, what would I be carrying?" He would say, "Nothing!" and blow a puff of air at me with a laugh!

Phonological Awareness and Reading

It is widely accepted that most children with reading difficulties have a core phonological deficit that interferes with their ability to develop phonological awareness, that is, the ability to perceive and manipulate the sounds of spoken words. Children who are learning to read differ widely in phonological awareness; some are very good at it by their second year in elementary school, while others at that age still find these simple games very difficult.

Phonological awareness has been repeatedly shown to be a strong predictor of reading ability, in both alphabetic and nonalphabetic writing systems. Studies have also shown that a child's level of phonological awareness, measured when reading instruction begins, accurately predicts his/her reading performance in later years. This holds true even after such variables as print exposure, letter knowledge, and verbal intelligence have been allowed for, and can be demonstrated as early as kindergarten. However, most researchers agree that phonological awareness alone does not account for all reading problems in children. Studies have shown that several cognitive processes are also good predictors of reading, at kindergarten and even before.

RAN: The Other Core Ability for Learning to Read

Recently, RAN has been acknowledged as a second core deficit in reading disabilities (see for example, Wolf and Bowers, 1999). RAN is described as the ability to name, as fast as possible, visually presented familiar symbols, such as colors, shapes, objects, and letters. It is the foundation for the skills of letter recognition, learning the sounds of words, and translating spelling to speech. As with phonological awareness, RAN performance has been shown to distinguish average from poor readers during childhood and into adulthood. Similarly, even after statistically equating IQ, reading experience, attention deficit disorder, socioeconomic status, articulation rate, and, most importantly, phonological awareness, RAN remains a reliable predictor of reading.

We know that naming of colors, shapes, and objects can significantly predict the naming of words. A recent study by Wolf and

Bowers (1999) offered some experimental evidence, demonstrating that the perception of objects and written words share some common features. These include grammatical encoding, phonological (syntactic) encoding, and articulation demand. The difference is that object recognition involves a semantic, or conceptual, system, whereas for naming written words, a syntactic system is sufficient. This study also suggested a theoretical reason for this common ground—object recognition and naming written words must share some fundamental cognitive process.

Tests of cognitive processes show that successive processing is central to early reading. It is significantly involved in word decoding, especially for pseudo-words and words to be read aloud (that is, requiring punctuation). Tasks testing successive processing correlate strongly with these basic reading requirements, the strongest correlations being those with the Speech Rate task (the fast repetition of three simple words), the Naming Time task (naming rows of single letters, digits, color strips, or simple and familiar words), and the Short-term Memory task. Simultaneous processing also plays an important part in basic reading skills, such as blending (in word reading) and comprehension of meaning. A consistent training program to enhance successive and simultaneous processing, independent of reading, can help children who are at risk for reading difficulties.

The importance of RAN in predicting reading ability and differentiating between poor and good readers has been shown not only in English, but also in languages characterized by a transparent orthography (for example, German, Dutch, or Greek). In languages other than English, it has been found that poor readers are more likely to have deficits in RAN than in phonological processing, and even in English, some poor readers with a speed deficit have no significant impairment in accurate reading of real or nonwords. It is widely accepted that the most severe kind of reading deficiency results from deficits in both speed and accuracy, as compared to individual readers who have only a speed deficit. In support of the unique contribution of RAN in predicting reading, Wolf and Bowers in their 1999 review paper suggested the double-deficit hypothesis (Wolf and Bowers, 1999). According to this hypothesis, four groups of children can be identified: a group with normal reading, a group with deficits only in rapid naming speed, a group with deficits only in phonological awareness, and a double-deficit group with difficulties in both RAN and phonological awareness. Children in the double-deficit group tend to have the most severe difficulties in learning to read. Several studies have found that children in the double-deficit group had the lowest scores on word identification, word attack, and reading comprehension measures, and also that children experiencing both phonological awareness and RAN deficits benefited the least from remediation.

Although RAN has been found to consistently account for variance in reading ability, the nature of the link between RAN and reading remains the focus of the ongoing debate. Various researchers have developed competing models to explain why RAN is related to reading. Some classify RAN as a type of phonological ability, maintaining that RAN tasks assess the rate of access to and retrieval of phonologically based information stored in long-term memory. Other researchers think that RAN should be considered a separate cognitive processing skill related to reading, asserting that RAN emphasizes skills like processing speed and the integration of visual processes with cognitive and linguistic processes.

Pause Time and Articulation Time

There is now ample evidence to show that successive processing difficulty is generally associated with reading difficulties in specifically reading-disabled children, but not in poor readers without such a disability. As we have seen, successive processing is important in reading, including in naming time.

Rapid automatic naming actually consists of several different tasks, and recent research shows that dyslexics perform differently from other poor readers. In a typical rapid naming time task, 40 or 50 randomly sequenced colors, pictures, numbers, or letters appear on a page in rows of 8 or 10 items. Time for rapid naming in these tasks can be divided into the time taken for the articulation of a letter (that is, searching for the name, assembling pronunciation, and actual articulation of the word) and the pause between articulating one item and the next. There may also be a significant pause between one set of items and the next. Recent research has shown that the major difference between dyslexic and nondyslexic readers exists in the pauses, rather than in the articulation time.

How can we explain pauses in terms of cognitive processes? The first component of the pause is disengagement of attention—the child has to give up what he has just said and get ready to say the name of the next color or letter. The remainder of the gap time could be broadly named encoding, which ends after finding a name for the next color, assembling the pronunciation for the color name, and forming a motor program for articulation. Each of these three different processes could contribute to the gap time. It is suggested that while repeating the stimuli over and over again (as in the typical naming time test of some 40 or 50 items), some amount of reactive inhibition may build up due to the continuous demand on fast reading. Reactive inhibition is expected to arise during massed practice (Eysenck, 1967). When this happens, involuntary rest pauses, a temporary condition of pauses, must occur for the dissipation of reactive inhibition. Therefore, perhaps towards the middle of the naming time task, reactive inhibition would be sufficiently strong to increase the gap time. Then, the child automatically takes an involuntary rest pause, becomes refreshed when the reactive inhibition has been dissipated, and comes back rejuvenated to resume at a faster naming speed.

An experiment by Georgiou and Parrila (2004) on kindergarten children reached a very interesting conclusion. The time to articulate the name of a color remained constant as children were observed from kindergarten through Grade 1, while the pause time was reduced. Notice that in the Figure E1, the two major components, articulation (the wavy and tall marks of speech) and pause time, are shown. In this case, a child is naming colors—*red, yellow, green, blue*. The pauses between the color naming and the articulation of the color name itself are distinctly visible in the diagram.

The children were tested three times, each time about 6 months apart—first in kindergarten, again in the fall term of Grade 1, and, finally, in the spring term of Grade 1. As the children got older, it was noticed that the articulation time hardly changes. The pause time,

Figure E1   Articulation and Pause Time

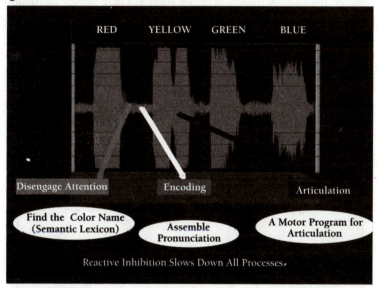

Source: Author.

however, was the longest in kindergarten, decreased substantially (by about 35 percent) 6 months later, and reduced further, though not so spectacularly, by the third test. The child is, perhaps, now able to encode faster, to disengage attention more efficiently, and to prepare for articulation by assembling a pronunciation that has become easier as he has grown older.

This research emphasizes the fact that speed is not a blanket term because even within the same task, the speed of articulation is unrelated to the pause time.

There are three important parts of reading (see Figure E2):

1. Phonology, that is, the sounds of letters, syllables, and words, when the sounds and syllables are blended. While reading a word, especially long and unfamiliar words, the sounds and syllables have to be segmented or broken apart.
2. Orthography, or the writing system that a language uses, which may give rise to confusion in reading words such as dead and bead, tough and though.

3. Semantics, or meaning of the words. The purpose of reading is not only to get sound from spelling, but also to get meaning from print.

Figure E2   Three Parts of Reading

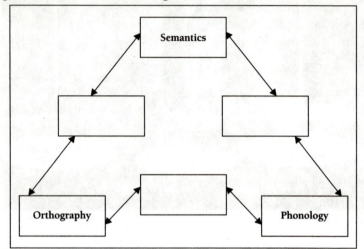

Source: Figure drawn by the author. Adapted from the Triangle Model of Seidenberg (2005).

Figure E2 is a simple model of the relationship among the three components given by Seidenberg (2005).

- The figure supports the observation that dyslexia is often associated with impairments in how the reader represents phonological information. If the representation is not accurate or weakened (degrading these representations), it is assumed to cause the reader to learn more slowly and to generalize reading poorly to similar words.
- The figure suggests that dyslexia can also have other causes. Many dyslexics show a general developmental delay in reading rather than a specific phonological deficit. What causes the delay?
- The figure suggests that this delay may arise from constitutional factors (for example, a learning deficit) or experiential ones

(for example, lack of reading experience). Some of these children may be "instructional dyslexics" who were taught using methods that did not include phonics.

- There are two main brain circuits involved in reading—a phonologically dominant one that develops earlier, and an orthography-semantics pathway that develops with additional experience as the child learns to read (Pugh et al., 2000).

- Where in the brain? Pugh and others demonstrated that on reading tasks that required phonological processing, such as determining if two made-up words rhyme (for example, *kime* and *nime*), normal readers showed a strong connection between two specific locations—the angular gyrus and other areas at the back of the left hemisphere. In contrast, dyslexics did not.

- However, normal readers and dyslexics showed similar connectivity between these areas on reading tasks that did not demand phonological processing.

- Such research implies that intact supporting neural connections can be utilized by dyslexics, if active phonological exercises (such as determining whether words rhyme, or identifying the first and last sounds in a word) are not demanded of them.

- Appropriate remediation or intervention programs (such as PREP, described earlier in the book) that do not teach phonics and do not require oral reading, but still enhance successive processing, can be effective in helping dyslexics become better readers.

- Successive processing contributes to understanding printed words and comprehending syntax.

- Can the PASS theory allow us to understand the difference between reading disabilities associated with a slow rate of word reading and those characterized by a high rate of phonological errors?

- Poor readers who are slow but not inaccurate should do poorly on the CAS successive processing test that demands articulation. This test requires rapid repetition of two or three simple words many times over. (for example, "Say the words *gauch lype* as fast as you can until I ask you to stop.")

- Slow, but accurate, readers should not perform poorly on other successive processing tests (for example, serial recall of words and sentences) that do not demand fast articulation. In contrast, those who are both slow and inaccurate readers should do poorly on all successive processing tests. This prediction is yet to be investigated.

Note of Acknowledgment: This chapter was written with invaluable inputs from George Georgiou. George is an Assistant Professor in Educational Psychology at the University of Alberta.

Notes

Chapter 1

The experts in the field of learning disability differ so much in their definitions of learning disability that it is impossible to cover it in one book. Learning disability covers such a broad range that it is almost a noninformative label for a parent or teacher of learning-disabled children, who is faced with their learning problems day in and day out. To make matters worse, some of the experts divide learning disability into disability that is seen in academic learning and disability that is seen in nonacademic learning. For example, where there are difficulties in reading, spelling, arithmetic, as well as in writing and composition, the label used is academic. These are separated from nonacademic disabilities that are apparently shown in visual-motor problems (such as in tying shoelaces, catching a ball, or phonological processing, as discussed in this chapter), memory problems, and even what are referred to as perceptual problems. The difficulty with these kinds of divisions, academic and nonacademic and further divisions within each—especially the nonacademic divisions comprising of visual-motor, perceptual, language, memory, and so on—is that the academic and nonacademic problems overlap to a very great extent. I have discussed this in Chapter 1 and, in fact, argued for a rational, yet commonsense, view of reading disability. Visual, spatial, perceptual, language, phonological, and memory processes—all these do affect reading, spelling, writing, and composition as well.

There is another difficulty with the use of the term learning disability along with reading disability. This concerns the label learning disability itself. In Britain, for example, mental retardation is now labelled as severe learning disability. In response to this, I have used the term dyslexia throughout the book.

One other important topic, popular in debates and arguments about dyslexia, has been omitted from this book. Strange as it may appear, there have been intermittent controversies with regard to the very existence of dyslexia. Some experts, again, advocate the view that it is curable, and thus it should not be recognized as a deficit. All through this book, however, we have presented this complex syndrome from various angles, especially from the point of view that it is a specific reading disability and a *cognitive difficulty*, that is, at least, associated with specific reading disability.

It is hoped that the line of association is a causal one; in other words, it is argued that the cognitive deficits in some way have contributed to the existence of specific reading disability. The best reference to familiarize the reader with some of the recent views regarding dyslexia is to be found in papers by Torgesen (1982; 1988).

Chapters 2 and 3

In these chapters, I have directly discussed phonological coding and its importance in learning to read. Along with this very important factor that contributes to reading disability, I have argued that there are cognitive processes that must be considered as well, when we go beyond phonological coding. These cognitive processes are discussed in detail in Chapter 4. In chapters 2 and 3, I try to demonstrate that dyslexia is a complex cognitive process, but it is also a complex neuropsychological process. The importance of neuropsychology in understanding dyslexia, and in designing remedial programs is discussed throughout the book. It is true that the brain functions, especially the organization in the cortex, might break down in specific ways in specific kinds of difficulty in dyslexia. The other important aspect in these chapters relates to the beginning of a discussion on comprehension, which is continued in Chapter 5. This chapter, along with Chapters 1 and 2, provides the groundwork for understanding dyslexia. Much further insight can be gained by reading the book by Harley (1995).

Whenever we describe something developing in stages, we are open to questions. Development is never linear and it seldom occurs in well-marked stages. So, what is the value of suggesting that reading occurs in stages? It is a convenient way of observing development, and it may be useful for locating the problems and doing what is necessary, if we are guided by a theory of stages of reading. Teachers and parents thus obtain a frame of reference for identifying children's reading difficulty by observing stages. Frith (1986, 1992) provides a reasoned discussion on stages.

Neuropsychology refers us back to the structure and functions of the brain, as these are constantly evolving with the cultural experiences of the individual. The new tools are the brain imaging techniques—CT scan, Magnetic Resonance Imaging, Positron Emission Tomography, and others. Posner and Raichle's book (1994) is a modern reference for connecting the brain to cognitive functions. It must be remembered, though, that the brain is a very complex organ and the experiences of the individual continuously shape and determine brain functions. Children differ from each other in the life experiences that affect their academic and nonacademic behaviors, along with their brain functions. So, let us not separate the mind from the physical structure!

Chapter 4

There are millions of children in the world who cannot read, not because they are dyslexic but because they are unschooled. Most of them grow up to be illiterate adults, and only a small percentage of the adults have the opportunity to enrol in reading classes for adult literacy. Do these children and adults who cannot read, lose a portion of their intelligence? They may think and reason differently from educated individuals, and lack of reading books and printed material may starve them of book-knowledge, but this should not turn them into unintelligent individuals. Here, we must distinguish the effect of schooling from the consequences of illiteracy. Schools provide a unique context for the development of mental functions of children. However much we may find faults with our schools, the culture of schooling promotes certain mental attitudes: the "schooled" mind regards a problem or its solution as one instance of a type of general problem or solution. Schooling also teaches us to "decontextualize" experiences, that is, to take the experience out of the immediate context. For example, Luria (1979) asked the illiterate peasants of Uzbekistan a reasoning question—Camels live where it is hot and dry, as in a desert. Berlin is a large city where it is very cold and wet. Would camels live there? The illiterate peasants could not accept the logical form of the statements, but had to refer to their experience. "I haven't seen Berlin but you say it is a large city; there may be camels, why not?"

Learning to read, certainly teaches children to pay attention to words and break the words down to phonemes and syllables. It also opens the world of print and writing to them. But lack of reading ability does not decrease their intelligence, unless we are testing for knowledge from books and the print media.

IQ may be irrelevant for determining who is reading-disabled, and it does not help us in remediation of reading disability. In fact, in remediating reading disability, the low-IQ children run the risk of being shortchanged. The teacher may either feel that children with low IQ cannot benefit from remediation or that resources can be better utilized for intelligent children who may be reading-disabled. However, some cognitive processes, especially when children are beginning to read, must play an important role as discussed in the chapter.

Chapter 5

The relevance of intelligence, as measured by IQ tests and the PASS cognitive processes, is clearly realized in children's ability for comprehension. It is not so surprising, as we read in the previous chapter, that IQ tests would predict a child's comprehension ability because the IQ test performance depends on school learning to a certain extent, and school learning depends on comprehension of the material in books.

We must separate word-decoding ability from comprehension, as even some children with mental retardation can learn to read well, but are limited in comprehension. Cognitive processes such as successive processing are obviously relevant for comprehension because if I forget the first part of a sentence while reading a long sentence, I cannot really understand it. So, in understanding syntax that leads to understanding a sentence, successive processing, that is, remembering the sequence of words, becomes absolutely necessary. Some children may have difficulties in reading comprehension, in which case we recommend listening comprehension for them; somebody must read to them as though they were blind and then check their comprehension, training in both decoding and comprehension is then recommended (see Chapters 7, 8, 9).

Chapter 6

Spelling and writing are really two separate skills; we can say that a child writes well, but makes many spelling errors. Most children, who speak their native language, already know its grammar by the time they enter school. Therefore some authorities in linguistics, such as Chomsky, believe that grammar is either innate or is the blueprint of the child's mind waiting to unfold. Grammar is universal in all languages; only their vocabulary is different. Whatever it may be, the children must learn to make their grammatical knowledge explicit as they learn to write. This can be a problem for many children—simply to place a period at the end of a sentence, for example, or a question mark at the end of a question, must be deliberately taught to children. The other problem in writing is that written sentences and paragraphs do not have voices that emphasize a certain point or intonations that express emotions; the written form is all we have. There is no environment or context we can depend upon as when we listen to a speaker. Writing must be explicit. See Olsen (1994) for further discussion.

However, do we not imagine a context or an environment in which the writing must be placed, so that we can understand it deeply? A successful reader not only reads the text, the written sentences or paragraphs, but also understands the subtext to get both the sense and meaning. Examples are given in this chapter, in chapter 5, and in chapter 16.

The next steps

On Writing

I asked my two granddaughters, "What is good writing?" Their answers were quite in line with what we generally know from research literature. A summary follows.

Silpi on Good Writing

(Silpi is 12 years and 2 months old. She is in Grade 7.)

"Must be creative. Must be thought out and logical. It must have a plan. Must use good vocabulary, grammar, etc."

Somya on Writing

(Somya is 7 years and 2 months old. She is in Grade 2.)

It must make sense. It shouldn't be boring. Must be interesting. While writing about something you must finish saying everything that you wish to say. Do not slip back to another idea. When other ideas that do not belong to the story come to your mind, keep them out. Write them as another story after you finish this one. You should use some big words such as *whispered, gigantic,* and *fantastic.* But do not use big words if you do not know their meaning.

Somya on the Difference Between Story and Essay

What is the difference between a story and an essay?
An essay?

Yes, like you write about something.

In a story? It must make sense. You must begin interestingly: Once upon a time there was a cat who met a wolf ... Then you go on writing, but you have to end it. When you have finished, you write The End.

So how do you write an essay?

Oh yes, we are studying about Japan. I can write about Japan. Their traditions and so on. When I have said what I know, I stop. I put a period. And that is the end.

Somya on Handwriting

What about handwriting, Somya? Now that computers are there to write, is good handwriting important?

Yes. You don't have to write beautiful handwriting but it should be neat. If it is so messy, no one can read what you have written. I watched a TV program exactly on this. There was this 7-year-old girl who didn't want to do handwriting. She wanted to write on the computer. Her mother said No! You have to do handwriting for half an hour. Then you can write on the computer.

Somya on Spelling

What about spelling? Does your writing have to have correct spelling?

No! If I am writing, and wish to write the word gigantic for example, I write it. My teacher then does not mind fixing up the spelling. Some children will stop and ask the teacher how to spell this or that word. They are wasting the teacher's time and they have stopped writing!

Comments by J.P. Das

The research literature seems to confirm the views of the two children on writing. Two essential components of writing are:

1. **Self-Regulation**

    (Planning, monitoring, evaluating, self-initiated thoughts, feelings, and actions.)

    * Goal setting and planning
    * Seeking information

- Record keeping, organizing, transforming (visualizing), and so on.
- Self-monitoring
- Self-evaluating
- Revising
- Self-verbalizing

2. **Transcription Skills**

- Spelling
- Handwriting

Note: Excerpted from Graham and Harris (2000).

The Vygotsky Framework—Social and Contextual View

Two major notions of Vygotsky (1978) are:

Inner Speech

Remember, one item is abbreviation of several connotations of words and sentences in external speech.

Scaffolding—Zone of Proximal Development and Use of Prompts

Remember, language comes to us populated—overpopulated—with the intention of others. Language we shape is the language that shapes us!

Comments by J.P. Das

Social environment and personal history together influence both the structure and the content of our writing; this follows from Vygotsky's notion. Children's written expressions develop within this context and, therefore, must vary with changes in the context. Formal instruction on writing, and the interactions with both peers and instructors, must also shape the written skills of a schoolchild. As always, writing is influenced by the perceived identity of the writer. However, writing skills go through peaks and valleys, but continue to grow throughout the child's developmental period and beyond.

Writing Development: What influences can we detect?

- Socio-historical context
- Local—writing at home, school, and on the bathroom wall differ!
- Classroom teaching
- Social interactions and collaborations
- Linked to social identity
- Writing development is nonlinear

Note: Excerpted from Schultz and Fecho (2000).

Chapter 7

Why remediation is not the same as instruction may not be immediately clear. Instruction for reading can be improved—divide instruction into several sessions of teaching; in each session, engage the students in activities that improve reading; as a teacher, participate in these activities as much as possible, and engage in direct teaching. Phonological skills can be taught in the reading instruction sessions. Improvement in reading should follow, but will not in case of children with dyslexia or specific reading disability. We need to examine the cognitive difficulties in these children, and we must do something about their learning the principles and general strategies they lack. While principles and general strategies are transferred to new situations, skills are not. Hence the emphasis on applying Vygotsky's notions of internalization and mediation (Das, 1995b).

Children must arrive at the essential principles and strategies by a sort of "guided discovery", having been exposed to the PREP training tasks, for example, and make these their own. Yes, we admit that instructing the whole class is cheaper than pulling out the learners with dyslexia and remediating individually or in small groups. But when our aim is to overcome specific reading deficits, the classroom instruction is not an option to consider. The concept of zone of proximal development discussed by Vygotsky (1978) provides a powerful rationale for expanding the learning potential of each child. For a discussion of the Vygotskian background, see several chapters in Lidz (1987).

Chapter 14

English as a second language (ESL)

Learning to read in English can be a challenge, because unlike the writing system of many other Indo-European languages, such as Oriya and Hindi, the sounds associated with particular letters in English are not entirely predictable. A recent report (Mishra and Stainthorp, 2007) focused on Oriya-speaking children educated in English-medium schools, who have been exposed to their mother tongue and speak it fluently. Their exposure to reading and writing in English began by kindergarten. Most of them were also introduced to reading and writing in Oriya during Grade 2 or 3, and possibly Hindi at the same time as well. The influence that such a multilingual literacy might have on English reading and comprehension was examined in a longitudinal study beginning at kindergarten. In fact, the objective of that project was to determine cross-linguistic development in reading. As the authors observed, learning to read English, consistently requires more fine-grained phonological analysis at the level of phonemes, than does learning to read Oriya. On the other hand, learning to speak, read, and write Oriya, equips children with the skills to analyze words at the level of syllables and words. Transfer across language, for ESL readers, does take place. Specifically, this is seen in phonological processing, verbal working memory, and syntactic skills. In addition, similar metacognitive strategies, such as planning and comprehension monitoring, and cognitive strategies, such as making inferences, are thought to be used by both monolingual and ESL readers during reading comprehension.

PREP improves information processing strategies, especially simultaneous and successive processing, as applied to the curriculum through PREP's bridging program.

Epilogue

Naming colors, letters, and digits, as fast as possible, is not a sign of speed of response, which in turn has been held as a biological measure of IQ. Let us understand "speed". Contrary to the claim that speed of processing is a basic component of intelligence, several studies have raised doubts about such a connection (Das, 2004). The vast literature on speed is mainly divided into two points of view. According to one, speed represents cognitive strategies that are specific to specific tasks, and for the other, speed is a general ability, a generic explanation for intelligence. What we suggest is that speed is not a good measure of IQ, unless we understand the cognitive processing that is measured by speed. This specific view of speed has two advantages. It defines processing, such as in PASS theory, in terms of certain kinds of tasks, and goes a step further. It is informative, with regard to the specific cognitive processes involved in performing those tasks. Such a domain-specific view of speed helps in understanding naming speed, a correlate of reading.

Figure N1 is one of the typical "speed of naming" tasks. This one is for naming letters as fast as possible. Obviously, the task is given to those children who can read letters of the alphabet quite well. The speed of reading from the first to the last letter is recorded. Research shows that compared to better readers, poor readers take a longer time to name the letters. Normally, we do not read a sentence or a word letter by letter. So why should a poor reader's rate of reading be slow? Because, the test is a test of the cognitive processes that determine reading speed, that is, those that contribute to the difference between individual readers. The text of the chapter contains a reasonable account of naming speed and its cognitive process companions.

Figure N1   Rapid Letter Naming

o	A	S	D	p	a	o	s	p	d
s	D	A	P	d	o	a	p	s	o
a	O	S	A	s	d	p	o	d	a
d	S	P	O	d	s	a	s	o	p
s	A	S	P	a	p	o	a	p	s

Source: Author.

Bibliography

Ashman, A.F. and R.M.F. Conway. 1997. *An Introduction to Cognitive Education: Theory and Applications*. London: Routledge.

Boden, C. and J.R. Kirby. 1995. 'Successive Processing, Phonological Coding and the Remediation of Reading', *Journal of Cognitive Education*, 4(2–3): 19–32.

Bowers, J.S., G. Vigliocco, H. Stadthagen-Gonzalez, and D. Vinson. 1999. 'Distinguishing Language from Thought: Experimental Evidence that Syntax Is Lexically rather than Conceptually Represented', *Psychological Science*, 10: 310–15.

Bradely, L. and P. Bryant. 1985. *Rhyme and Reason in Reading and Spelling*. Ann Arbor: University of Michigan Press.

Burgess, N. and G. Hitch. 1999. 'Memory for Serial Order: A Network Model of Phonological Loop and its Timing', *Psychological Review*, 103: 551–81.

Carlson, J. and J.P. Das. 1998. 'A Process Approach to Remediating Word-Decoding Deficiencies in Chapter I Children', *Learning Disability Quarterly*, 20: 93–102.

Coltheart, M., K. Rastle, C. Perry, R. Langdon, and J. Ziegler. 2001. 'DRC: A Dual Route Cascaded Model of Visual Word Recognition and Reading Aloud', *Psychological Review*, 108: 204–56.

Cromier, P., J.S. Carlson, and J.P. Das. 1990. 'Planning Ability and Cognitive Performance: The Compensatory Effects of a Dynamic Assessment Approach', *Learning and Individual Differences*, 2: 437–49.

Das, J.P. 1973. 'Cultural Deprivation and Cognitive Competence', in N.R. Ellis (ed.), *International Review of Research in Mental Retardation*, pp. 2–53. New York: Academic Press.

———. 1995a. 'Is there Life after Phonological Coding?', *Issues in Education*, 1: 87–90.

———. 1995b. 'Some Thoughts on Two Aspects of Vygotsky's Work', *Educational Psychologist*, 30: 93–97.

———. 1998. *The Working Mind*. New Delhi: Sage.

———. 1999. *PREP: PASS Reading Enhancement Program*. Edmonton: Development Disabilities Centre, University of Alberta, Canada.

———. 2004. *The Cognitive Enhancement Training Program (COGENT©)*. Edmonton: Developmental Disabilities Centre, AB: University of Alberta.

Das, J.P., D. Hayward, S. Samantaray, and J.J. Panda. 2006. 'Cognitive Enhancement Training (COGENT): What Is It? How Does it Work With a Group of Disadvantaged Children?', *Journal of Cognitive Education and Psychology*, 5: 328–35.

Das, J.P., B.C. Kar, and R.K. Parrila. 1996. *Cognitive Planning: The Psychological Basis of Intelligent Behaviour*. New Delhi: Sage.

Das, J.P., J.R. Kirby, and R.F. Jarman. 1975. 'Simultaneous and Successive Syntheses: An Alternative Model for Cognitive Abilities', *Psychological Bulletin*, 82: 87–103.

———. 1979. *Simultaneous and Successive Cognitive Processes*. New York: Academic Press.

Das, J.P., D.L. Mensink, and R.K. Mishra. 1990. 'Cognitive Processes Separating Good and Poor Readers when IQ Is Covaried', *Learning and Individual Differences*, 2: 423–36.

Das, J.P., R.K. Mishra, and J.E. Pool. 1995. 'An Experiment in Cognitive Remediation of Word-Reading Difficulty', *Journal of Learning Disabilities*, 28: 66–79.

Das, J.P. and J.A. Naglieri. 1993. *Das-Naglieri: Cognitive Assessment System (DN-CAS)*. Standardized edition. Itasca, Illinios: Riverside.

Das, J.P., J.A. Naglieri, and J.R. Kirby. 1994. *Assessment of Cognitive Processes: The PASS Theory of Intelligence*. Boston: Allyn & Bacon.

Das, J.P., R.K. Parrila, and T.C. Papadopoulus. 2000. 'Cognitive Education and Reading Disability', in A. Kozulin, and Y. Rand (eds), *Experience in Mediated Learning*. London: Elsevier.

Eysenck, H.J. 1967. *The Biological Basis of Personality*. Springfield, IL: Thomas.

Fodor, J.A. 1983. *Modularity of Mind*. Cambridge, Mass.: MIT Press.

Frith, U. 1985. 'Beneath the Surface of Developmental Dyslexia', in K.E. Patterson, J.C. Marshall, and M. Coltheart (eds), *Surface Dyslexia*. Hove, UK: Erlbaum.

———. 1986. 'A Developmental Framework for Developmental Dyslexia', *Annals of Dyslexia*, 36: 69–81.

———. 1992. 'Cognitive Development and Cognitive Deficit', *The Psychologist: Bulletin of the British Psychological Society*, 5: 13–19.

———. 1999. 'Paradoxes in the Definition of Dyslexia', *Dyslexia*, 5: 192–214.

Gal'perin, P.Y. 1982. 'Intellectual Capabilities among Older Preschool Children: On the Problem of Training and Mental Development', in W.W. Hartup (ed.), *International Review of Child Development*, pp. 526–46. Chicago: Chicago University Press.

Gathercole, S.E. and A.D. Baddley. 1989. 'The Role of Phonological Memory in Normal and Disordered Language Development', in C. von Euler, I. Lundberg, and G. Lennestrand (eds), *Brain and Reading*, pp. 245–55. New York: Macmillan.

Georgiou, G. and R. Parrila. 2004. 'RAN Components and Reading Acquisition', paper presented to annual conference at Society for the Scientific Study of Reading Conference, Amsterdam, June.

Graham, S. and K.R. Harris. 2000. 'The Role of Self-regulation and Transcription Skills in Writing and Writing Development', *Educational Psychologist*, 35: 3–12.

Harley, T.A. 1995. *The Psychology of Language*. Hove, UK: Erlbaum.

Harm, W. and M.S. Seidenberg. 1999. 'Phonology, Reading Acquisition, and Dyslexia: Insights from Connectionist Models', *Psychological Review*, 106: 491–528.

Hayward, D., J.P. Das, and T. Janzen. 2007. 'Innovative Programs for Improvement in Reading through Cognitive Enhancement', *Journal of Learning Disabilities*, 40: 443–57.

Haywood, H.C. and J.T. Tapp. 1966. 'Experience and Development of Adaptive Behaviour', in N.R. Ellis (ed.), *International Review of Research in Mental Retardation*, pp. 109–51. New York: Academic Press.

Just, M.A. and P.A. Carpenter. 1977. *Cognitive Processes in Comprehension*. Hillsdale, NJ: Erlbaum.

Kar, B.C., U.N. Dash, J.P. Das, and J.S. Carlson. 1992. 'Two Experiments on the Dynamic Assessment of Planning', *Learning and Individual Differences*, 5: 13–29.

Karmiloff-Smith, A. 1992. *Beyond Modularity: A Developmental Perspective on Cognitive Science*. Cambridge, Mass.: MIT Press.

Kirby, J.R., C.A. Booth, and J.P. Das. 1996. 'Cognitive Processes and IQ in Reading Disability', *Journal of Special Education*, 29: 442.

Kirby, J.R. and N.H. Williams. 1991. *Learning Problems: A Cognitive Approach*. Toronto: Kagan & Woo.

Kuhl, P. 2000. 'Language, Mind and the Brain: Experience Alters Perception', in M.S. Gazzaniga (ed.), *The New Cognitive Neuroscience*, pp. 99–115. Cambridge, Mass.: MIT Press.

Kuhn, D. 1995. 'Micro-genetic Study of Change—What it Has Told Us', *Psychological Science*, 6: 133–39.

Lidz, C.S. (ed.). 1987. *Dynamic Assessment: An Interactional Approach to Evaluating Learning Potential*. New York: Guildford Press.

Lundberg, I., J. Frost, and O.P. Petersen. 1988. 'Effects of an Extensive Program for Stimulating Phonological Awareness in Preschool Children', *Reading Research Quarterly*, 23: 263–84.

Luria, A.R. 1963. *Restoration of Function after Brain Injury*. B. Haigh (trans.), O.L. Zangwill (ed.). New York: Macmillan.

———. 1966a. *Higher Cortical Functions in Man*. London: Tavistock.

———. 1966b. *Human Brain and Psychological Processes*. New York: Harper & Row.

———. 1973. *The Working Brain: An Introduction to Neuropsychology*. New York: Basic Books.

———. 1979. *The Making of Mind*. Cambridge, Mass.: Harvard University Press.

———. 1981. *Language and Cognition*. New York: John Wiley and Sons Inc.

Mahapatra, S. and U.N. Dash. 1999. 'Reading Achievement in Relation to PASS Processes', in U.N. Dash and U. Jain (eds), *Perspectives on Psychology and Social Development*. New Delhi: Concept Publishing Company.

McCarthy, R.A. and E.K. Warrington. 1990. *Cognitive Neuropsychology: A Clinical Introduction*. New York: Academic Press.

Mishra, R. and R. Stainthorp. 2007. 'The Relationship between Phonological Awareness and Word Reading Accuracy in Oriya and English: A Study of Oriya-speaking Fifth-graders', *Journal of Research in Reading*, 30: 23–37.

Mohanty, N. 2007. *Psychological Disorder: Text and Cases*. Hyderabad: Neelkamal Publications.

Morris, R.D., K.K. Stuebing, J.M. Fletcher, S.E. Shaywitz, G.R. Lyon, D.P. Shankweiler, L. Katz, D.J. Francis, and B.A. Shaywitz. 1998. 'Subtypes of Reading Disability: Variability around a Phonological Core', *Journal of Educational Psychology*, 90: 347–73.

Naglieri, J.A. 1999. *Essentials of CAS Assessment*. New York: John Wiley.

Naglieri, J.A. and J.P. Das. 1987. 'Construct and Criterion-related Validity of Planning, Simultaneous and Successive Cognitive Processing Tasks', *Journal of Psychoeducational Assessment*, 4: 353–63.

————. 1997. *Das-Naglieri Cognitive Assessment System Interpretive Handbook*. Chicago: Riverside.

Naglieri, J.A. and S.H. Gottling. 1997. 'Mathematics Instruction and PASS Cognitive Processes: An Intervention Study', *Journal of Learning Disabilities*, 30: 513–20.

Naglieri, J.A. and D. Johnson. 2000. 'Effectiveness of a Cognitive Strategy Intervention in Improving Arithmetic Computation based on the PASS Theory', *Journal of Learning Disabilities*, 33: 591–97.

Olsen, D. 1994. *The World on Paper*. Cambridge: Cambridge University Press.

Papadopoulus, T.C., R.K. Parrila, and J.R. Kirby. 1998. *Predictors of Reading Development in At-risk Children: A Longitudinal Study*. Edmonton: Developmental Disabilities Centre, University of Alberta.

Parrila, R.K., J.P. Das, M.E. Kendrick, T.C. Papadopoulus, and J.R. Kirby. 1999. 'Efficacy of a Cognitive Reading Remediation Program for At-risk Children in Grade 1', *Developmental Disabilities Bulletin*, 27: 1–31.

Parrila, R.K. and J.R. Kirby. 2000. 'Naming Speed, Articulation Rate and STM as Predictors of Poor and Normal Development', paper read at Society for the Scientific Study of Reading Conference, Stockholm.

Patton, H.D., J.W. Sundsten, W.E. Crill, and P.D. Swanson. 1976. *Introduction to Basic Neurology*. Philadelphia: Saunders.

Paulesu, E., J.R. Demonet, F. Fazio, E. McCrory, V. Chanoine, N. Bunswick, S.F. Cappa, G. Cossu, M. Habib, C.D. Frith, and U. Frith. 2001. 'Dyslexia: Cultural Diversity and Biological Unity', *Science*, 291: 2165–67.

Paulesu, E., E. McCrory, F. Fazio, L. Menoncello, N. Brunswick, S.F. Cappa, M. Cotelli, G. Cossu, F. Corte, M. Lorusso, S. Pesenti, A. Gallagher, D. Perani, C. Price, C.D. Frith, and U. Frith. 2000. 'A Cultural Effect on Brain Function', *Nature Neuroscience*, 3: 91–96.

Pollasteck, A. and K. Rayner. 1993. 'Reading', in M.I. Posner (ed.), *Foundations of Cognitive Science*, pp. 401–36. Cambridge, Mass.: MIT Press.

Posner, M.I. and M.E. Raichle. 1994. *Images of Mind*. New York: Scientific American Library.

Pugh, K.R., W. Einar Mencl, B.A. Shaywitz, R.K. Fulbright, R.T. Constable, P. Skudlarski, K.E. Marchione, A.R. Jenner, J.M. Fletcher, A.M. Liberman, D.P. Ahnkweiler, L. Katz, C. Lacadie, and J.C. Gore. 2000. 'The Angular Gyrus in Developmental Dyslexia: Task-specific Differences in Functional Connectivity within Posterior Cortex', *Psychological Science*, 11: 52–56.

Rushdie, S. 1991. *Haroun and the Sea of Stories*. New Delhi: Penguin.

Schmeck, R.R. 1988. *Learning Strategies and Learning Styles*. New York: Plenum Press.

Schultz, K. and B. Fecho. 2000. 'Society's Child: Social Context and Writing Development', *Educational Psychologist*, 35: 31–62.

Seidenberg, M.S. 2005. 'Connectionist Models of Word Reading', *Current Directions in Psychological Science*, 14: 238–42.

Share, D.L. and K.E. Stanovich. 1995. 'Cognitive Processes in Early Reading Development: Accommodating Individual Differences into a Model of Acquisition', *Issues in Education: Contributions for Educational Psychology*, 1: 1–57.

Siegler, R.S. and K. Crowley. 1991. 'The Microgenetic Method', *American Psychologist*, 46: 606–20.

Stanovich, K.E. 1988. 'Explaining the Differences between Dyslexic and the Garden-variety Poor Reader: The Phonological Core-variable Difference Model', *Journal of Learning Disabilities*, 21: 590–604.

Stein, D.G. 1988. 'In Pursuit of New Strategies for Understanding Recovery from Brain Damage: Problems and Perspectives', in T. Boll and B.K. Bryant (eds), *Clinical Neuropsychology and Brain Function: Research, Measurement and Practice*. Washington DC: American Psychological Association.

Tolstoy, L. 1967. 'The Death of Ivan Ilych', in *Great Short Works of Leo Tolstoy*. New York: Harper & Row.

———. 2002. *Anna Karenina*. New York: Penguin.

Torgesen, J.K. 1982. 'The Use of Rationally Defined Subgroups in Research on Learning Disabilities', in J.P. Das, R.R. Mulcahy, and A.E. Wall (eds), *Theory and Research in Learning Disabilities*, pp. 111–31. New York: Plenum Press.

———. 1988. 'Studies of Children with Learning Disabilities who Perform Poorly on Memory Span Tasks', *Journal of Learning Disabilities*, 21, 605–12.

———. 2002. 'Lessons Learned from Intervention Research in Reading: Away to Go before We Rest', in R. Stainthorpe (ed.) *Learning and Teaching Reading: British Journal of Educational Psychology Monograph Series II*, 1(1): 89–104.

Torgesen, J.K. and G. Houck. 1980. 'Processing Deficiencies in Learning Disabled Children Who Perform Poorly on the Digit Span Task', *Journal of Educational Psychology*, 72: 141–60.

Torgesen, J.K. C.A. Rashotte, J. Greestein, G. Houck, and P. Portes. 1987. 'Academic Difficulties of Learning-disabled Children Who Perform Poorly on Memory Span Tasks', in H.L. Swanson (ed.), *Memory and Learning Disabilities: Advances in Learning and Behavioural Disabilities*. Greenwich, CT: JAI Press.

Torgesen, J.K., R.K. Wagner, and C.A. Rashotte. 1994. 'Longitudinal Studies of Phonological Processing and Reading', *Journal of Learning Disabilities*, 27: 276–86.

Vygotsky, L.S. 1962. *Thought and Language*. Cambridge, Mass.: MIT Press.

———. 1978. *Mind in Society: The Development of Higher Psychological Processes*. Cambridge, Mass.: Harvard University Press.

———. 1986. *Thought and Language* (translation newly revised and edited by Alex Kozulin). Cambridge, Mass.: MIT Press.

Wechsler, D. 1974. *Wechsler Intelligence Scale for Children* (Revised). New York: Psychological Corp.

Wolf, M. and P. Greig Bowers. 1999. 'The Double-deficit Hypothesis for the Developmental Dyslexias', *Journal of Educational Psychology*, 91: 415–38.

Woodcock, R.W. 1987. *Woodcock Reading Mastery Tests—Revised*. Circle Pines, MN: American Guidance Service.

Ziegler, J. and U. Goswami. 2005. 'Reading Acquisition, Developmental Dyslexia, and Skilled Reading across Languages: A Psycholinguistic Grain Size Theory', *Psychological Bulletin*, 131(1): 3–29.

About the Author

J.P. Das is Emeritus Professor of Educational Psychology and Emeritus Director of the J.P. Das Developmental Disabilities Centre at the University of Alberta, Edmonton, Canada where currently he is a research professor. He obtained an honors degree in Philosophy and a Master of Arts in Experimental Psychology in India as well as a PhD in Psychology from the University of London Institute of Psychiatry, working with Hans Eysenck. His research on understanding cognitive psychology has resulted in several scholarly books, including: *Verbal Conditioning and Behaviour* (1969); *Simultaneous and Successive Processes* (with J.R. Kirby and R.F. Jarman, 1979); *Assessment of Cognitive Processes: The PASS Theory of Intelligence* (with J.A. Naglieri and J.R. Kirby, 1994); *Cognitive Planning* (with B.C. Kar and R.K. Parrila, 1996); and *The Working Mind* (1998). The Chinese translation of *Assessment of Cognitive Processes* was published in 1999, and the Chinese version of this book was published in 2007. He has published some 250 research papers and book chapters, many of which have focused on efforts to redefine intelligence. He has held visiting appointments at Peabody College, Vanderbilt University (as a Kennedy Foundation Professor); the University of California, Los Angeles; Monash University in Melbourne, Australia; and Moscow State University. Dr Das and his co-author, Dr Jack Naglieri, have produced the Das-Naglieri Cognitive Assessment System (CAS), published in 1997 (now translated and normed in Italian, Japanese, Korean, Norwegian, and Spanish). In 1999 Dr Das was inducted as a Fellow of the Royal Society, Canada, for his original contribution to the field of intelligence.